SCOTTISH SHORTS

Related Titles Published by Nick Hern Books

SCOT FREE
ed. Alastair Cameron

John Byrne
WRITER'S CRAMP

John Clifford
LOSING VENICE

Anne Marie Di Mambro
THE LETTER BOX

Chris Hannan
ELIZABETH GORDON QUINN

John McKay
DEAD DAD DOG

Rona Munro
SATURDAY AT THE COMMODORE

Tony Roper
THE STEAMIE

SCOTLAND PLAYS
ed. Philip Howard

Catherine Czerkawska
WORMWOOD

Ann Marie Di Mambro
BROTHERS OF THUNDER

Stephen Greenhorn
PASSING PLACES

David Greig
ONE WAY STREET

Liz Lochhead
QUELQUES FLEURS

Linda McLean
ONE GOOD BEATING

Iain Crichton Smith
LAZYBED

SCOTTISH SHORTS

DAVEY ANDERSON ▪ SNUFF

CATHERINE CZERKAWSKA ▪ THE PRICE OF A FISH SUPPER

STANLEY EVELING ▪ BETTER DAYS BETTER KNIGHTS

DAVID GREIG ▪ RAMALLAH

DAVID HARROWER ▪ 54% ACRYLIC

DOUGLAS MAXWELL ▪ HARM

RONA MUNRO ▪ THE BASEMENT FLAT

MORNA PEARSON ▪ DISTRACTED

LOUISE WELSH ▪ THE IMPORTANCE OF BEING ALFRED

Selected and introduced by Philip Howard

NICK HERN BOOKS

London

www.nickhernbooks.co.uk

A Nick Hern Book

Scottish Shorts first published in Great Britain in 2010 as a paperback original by Nick Hern Books Limited, 14 Larden Road, London W3 7ST

Snuff copyright © 2010 Davey Anderson
The Price of a Fish Supper copyright © 2010 Catherine Czerkawska
Better Days Better Knights copyright © 2010 Estate of Stanley Eveling
Ramallah copyright © 2010 David Greig
54% Acrylic copyright © 2010 David Harrower
Harm copyright © 2010 Douglas Maxwell
The Basement Flat copyright © 2010 Rona Munro
Distracted copyright © 2010 Morna Pearson
The Importance of Being Alfred copyright © 2010 Louise Welsh
Introduction copyright © 2010 Philip Howard

The authors have asserted their moral rights

Cover designed by Ned Hoste, 2H
Cover image © iStockphoto.com

Typeset by Nick Hern Books, London
Printed and bound in Great Britain by CPI Bookmarque, Croydon, Surrey

A CIP catalogue record for this book is available from the British Library

ISBN 978 1 84842 070 0

Contents

Introduction

Philip Howard

Of the nine plays in this collection, seven date from the decade 2000–09, a decade that saw two distinct developments in the evolution of Scottish theatre. One is a big cultural statement and represents a millennial shift in thinking – the founding of the National Theatre of Scotland; the other is a bubbling undercurrent – the emergence of a thriving, idiosyncratic subculture of one-act plays, centring on the lunchtime series at the Òran Mór venue in Glasgow. Of course it is foolhardy to attempt to analyse such modern history, but there is a perception, albeit anecdotal, that the latter half of the decade witnessed a wane in the celebrated boom in Scottish playwriting that had started in the 1990s. The truth is rather that the talent is there – you just have to start looking for it in different places.

The long-running campaign for the establishment of a national theatre for Scotland now feels, in retrospect, like a miniature version within the cultural sector of the twentieth-century struggle for the re-establishment of a Scottish Parliament. Within the first year of that Parliament, the publication of a National Cultural Strategy in 2000 committed the new Scottish Executive to developing a National Theatre organisation, and by the autumn of 2003 the finance was confirmed for it to proceed. The new National Theatre of Scotland is both a symbolic and actual demonstration of the confidence of the theatre culture here. Under its founding Artistic Director, Vicky Featherstone, its repertoire is firmly forward-looking in the mould of a new-writing theatre, as displayed triumphantly in its greatest (and global) success thus far, Gregory Burke and John Tiffany's *Black Watch* (2006): a delicious rebuff both to the dying generation that believed a Scottish national theatre must devote itself to a parade of the hundred loftiest revivals, but also to those of us naysayers who obstinately believed there needn't be a national theatre institution in Scotland at all.

Meanwhile, far below the radar of public funding, in a model of disestablishment, there is the A Play, a Pie and a Pint programme of short plays at Òran Mór, Glasgow, founded in 2004 by producer/director David MacLennan, graduate of 7:84 Theatre Company and brave-hearted Scottish cultural warrior. MacLennan's original inspiration for this project was a visit to Cuba, where he noticed that the cane sugar workers on the *bateyes* (plantations) always listened to jazz of conspicuous quality while they worked, and he came back to Scotland with a mission to bring that level of endemic, daily – or at least weekly – cultural experience to the office workers of Glasgow's West End.

This series, which, at the time of writing, is just about to produce its two-hundredth world premiere, has had an astonishing impact on Scottish theatre, providing a unique training ground for emerging writers and directors, and becoming the largest de facto commissioning body for playwrights in Scotland. For approximately forty weeks in the year, in a converted church complex – which now feels like a secular cathedral – audiences can see a different play each week, with a pie and a drink thrown in for good measure. By no means are all the plays good, and the dramaturgical processes are variable, but audiences come in their droves, partly as a response to MacLennan's deft showmanship, and partly because they are willing to take the risk on a theatre visit which doesn't require much investment of time or money. And the writers? Well, for them too, the risk of creating a new piece of work is similarly reduced. As the critic Joyce McMillan succinctly puts it, 'the addition of the pie enshrines their right to fail'. The Òran Mór project, whether by accident or design, has identified a whole new generation of Scottish playwrights that might have been shy of a commission from an established new-writing theatre, but also allows more seasoned playwrights to try something formally different, or writers in another field, such as the novelist Louise Welsh, to start writing for the stage.

The Importance of Being Alfred by Louise Welsh (Òran Mór, Glasgow, 2005), which has already been revived several times since its premiere at A Play, a Pie and a Pint, proposes a

meeting between an ageing Lord Alfred Douglas and Noel
Pemberton Billing (1881–1948), the Boer War veteran, boxer,
airman, Independent MP, occasional playwright, professional
homophobe and outrageous conspiracy theorist. However, the
play's antagonist is not Billing, but Bosie, Alfred Douglas's
younger self, and what follows is a hilarious and yet terrifying
comedy of manners, which conceals a profound platonic
dialogue between Alfred and Bosie, between A and B,
between the two halves of the self; meanwhile Pemberton
Billing, the tritagonist, blusters and embellishes and stokes the
fire.

This is Welsh's first play but she meets the challenge of the
short-play form head-on. She doesn't try and nail the drama to
the revelation that Alfred and Bosie are two versions of the same
self – there is a hint even by the sixth line of the play – her
triumph is rather to find the right language for a meeting of three
such characters, no mean feat in the setting of a 1918
gentleman's study, dressed with antimacassars, and brimming
with fear and loathing. The language seems perfectly poised
between ancient and modern, Wildean in its elegance but not
florid. She doesn't try to resist the occasional double entendre
but the overall effect is of surprising restraint – presumably so as
not to shift focus from the hefty emotional undertow of Alfred
and Bosie's confrontation. Similarly, while there is comedy in
the fact that Billing can't see Bosie, and that Alfred is squirming
at Bosie's interventions, Bosie is no blithe spirit and there is no
farce with ghostly flying whisky glasses to distract from Welsh's
serious purpose. Her coup is merely the revelation that the divide
of the self is more complex than we have been thinking, and the
argument not as one-sided. Finally, in a masterstroke of Queer
theatre, Welsh enjoys a tantalising glimpse of the erotic
attraction between Alfred and his younger self.

The Price of a Fish Supper by Catherine Czerkawska (Òran
Mór, Glasgow, 2005) is the only monologue drama, from a
crowded field, included in this volume. Czerkawska's anti-hero
is Rab, a forty-something ex-seaman who still sweats salt water
from every pore, despite having been left high and dry by pretty
much everything in his life: thwarted love, fraternal rivalry, and

a fishing industry on the Ayrshire coast and lower Clyde in terminal decline. Czerkawska knows and understands the maritime life of her character closely – 'the sea's in my head' – and the central story of the play is loosely based on a real incident in 1990 when the nets of the fishing vessel *Antares* snagged on the submarine *HMS Trenchant* in the Sound of Bute, leading to the loss of all four crew's lives.

The play belongs obliquely in the very British genre of 'work plays', where a workplace or industry provide a setting or driving theme – but only in an ironic way because of course here the point is that the industry has rendered Rab a fish out of water; or, as the locals call him, a 'shore skipper'. It's not unusual in this genre for a character to testify to the decline of their industry or livelihood, but Czerkawska goes much deeper in relating the fortunes of the industry and the character to one another. Rab insists that the difference between fishermen and farmers or miners is that the latter two have fought the decline of their industry harder or more successfully. 'The price of fish' is both the hard single economic fact that informs every word of the drama, but also a poetic refrain throughout it.

Czerkawska is careful to avoid sentimentalising Rab's predicament, and much of the drama of the piece is carried by his wonderfully sardonic, un-self-pitying commentary: he wryly remarks that the cost of entry to the maritime museum is the price of a fish supper. By the end of the play Rab knows that it's not just the waters off Carrick, but also himself, that are now 'overfished' – although, in the closing moments, the decline of the industry and of the character are momentarily disentangled, as Rab glimpses a beacon of hope.

54% Acrylic by David Harrower is a radio play from 1998 which was nominated for a Sony Award. A version for the stage was produced at Òran Mór, Glasgow, in 2006. In some ways it is a companion piece to Harrower's second stage play, *Kill the Old Torture Their Young* (Traverse, Edinburgh), also from 1998, in that they both attempt to get to grips with the isolationism of contemporary urban life – in direct contrast to Harrower's globally successful first play, *Knives in Hens*, with its striking pre-industrial setting.

Here Harrower adroitly fits the story to the medium: Marion, a nineteen-year-old girl, covets a green dress in a department store, and Gerry the security guard monitors her progress from ingénue to shoplifter. Marion escapes with the dress and Gerry gives chase: 'We are the hunters and they are the hunted.' The text moves energetically from monologue testimony to the audience, to direct speech between Marion and Gerry; and, throughout, a faceless Security Supervisor's orders to Gerry (via his radio) accord an extra aural texture, complete with walkie-talkie crackle. When Gerry follows Marion across the river, in his now obsessive determination to trap his prey, he disobeys the Supervisor's order to come back into the store, back from the world outside, where you will lose radio contact and where 'you're on your own'.

With careful editing, Harrower makes it into a thriller of miniscule detail, and his empathy with the characters is complete: when Marion starts the long journey from the floor where she has stuffed the dress into her zipped-up jacket – down the escalator – towards the exit – she is at first alarmed and dazzled by the brightness of the sun of the world through the glass doors. He notes Marion's own fascination with the gorgeous but supercilious shop assistant that condescends towards her so infuriatingly. But the main thrust of the play has to be the strange dance that plays out between shoplifter and security guard (Gerry: 'They can sense us, who we are, as much as we sense them'). Maybe, at the beginning of the play, we could see that Gerry's initial suspicion of Marion was based not so much on a 'hunch', as he describes it, but on an erotic attraction – but it's only here, at the end, that we realise Harrower has duped us all along, and that we've been witnessing an entirely original love story.

Davey Anderson's *Snuff* was premiered at the Arches, Glasgow, in 2005 before transferring to the Traverse for the Edinburgh Festival in the same year, and subsequently to London at Theatre503, with support from the new National Theatre of Scotland. He keeps us guessing as to whether or not Kevin, the protagonist of the play, is a veteran of the Bush/Blair wars in Iraq and Afghanistan, as his 'pal' Billy is, or indeed whether he's been a serving soldier at all; but, either way, it seems, somehow, to spur this deep and concentrated portrait of paranoia. Anderson keeps the tension at almost permanent red alert by constantly shifting the possibilities of what exactly the clear and present danger is. We cannot be sure of the fate of Kevin's sister Pamela, who remains a haunting offstage presence and frequent on-screen one in Kevin's video assemblage: are we watching a play called *Snuff* or a snuff movie? And the sparring between Kevin and Billy, which often resembles a malign vaudeville double-act, never relaxes for a second. One of the few certainties in the play is the deprivation of the block in which Kevin festers, a block so broken that, just as Kevin was sure that he, the last resident, would be detonated in it, so it became an ideal home for a new community of immigrants and asylum-seekers.

Anderson succeeds in relating the unparalleled experience of modern war in Iraq with an everyday experience of urban strife and paranoia. Kevin is so preoccupied with the idea of surveillance that he has amassed his own library of videotapes. The story that Billy relates of how they used to torture the 'darkie' kid in school feels like a rehearsal for Iraq; Kevin pairs this with an anecdote about the family downstairs being broken into – we can't be sure if it was him or not – and facing 'GO HOME' graffitied on the wall. We also learn that Billy is not immune from battle damage through his dreamscape of a burqa-shrouded Afghan woman morphing into a naked Pamela. And when Kevin dresses his temporary hostage Billy in a Guantanamo-style orange boiler suit ('Mister Orange'), we sense this resonates with his declared Unionist/Rangers/Orange credentials. It may be Glasgow, but it's still a war.

Rona Munro's *The Basement Flat* was commissioned for the Traverse's enterprising 'The World is Too Much' breakfast series at the 2009 Edinburgh Festival. Munro scores a bull's-eye in meeting the key demand of a very short play: to create the most complete world in the quickest time. Much of the drama rests on the interplay between the known and the unknown or unknowable: Fiona and Stephen are instantly recognisable, their concerns are our concerns, but the unseen man who paces the

floor above their heads is a mass of contradictions whose very
elusiveness threatens their peace. He is both benign neighbour
and feudal landlord; where he once tended his window boxes he
now plans to build a security fence, and wields a gun. And their
daughter Susan is metamorphosing from truculent teen back to
feral child, and now – in an image worthy of Ovid or a pre-
Raphaelite painting – is running with the foxes, her copper hair
matching their pelt.

Munro reinvents the idea of suburbia: Fiona covets a patio,
an olive tree and a Cath Kidston apron, and yet the bricks and
mortar of their house sit at the vanguard of a war with nature.
The cultivated ivy in the window boxes has died, the walls are
cracking and there is a damp patch in the shape of a whale in
the living room; but outside, the wild ivy is climbing down the
chimney, the lawn has grown unmowable, the pavements have
greened over – and all the while their vulpine daughter is
scraping away at the mortar in a bid to destroy the house. In
Munro's vision, it's almost as if the children are the only ones
who realise that the game's a bogey, and a return to nature the
only possible end to the story of humankind.

When Morna Pearson burst on to the playwriting scene in
Scotland with her one-act play *Distracted* in 2006, which
premiered as part of a triple bill of new voices at the Traverse
entitled *Tilt*, it felt almost as if a new genre had been born, a
genre of Doric surrealism, if that isn't too arcane a concept.
Pearson was raised in Elgin, Morayshire, and this provides an
approximate setting for the caravan park in the play. She seizes
the dialect Scots of North East Scotland, normally associated, in
a literary context at least, with an earthy, rural but somehow
respectful atavism, and gives it a thorough kicking: 'Saturday
Nicht's Alricht for Fichting'. The blend of the Doric, the trashy
1980's song titles, the Latin genus names of Jamie Purdy's
entomological surveys, and the wild flights of fancy, makes for
a sublime originality.

Pearson is relatively disinterested in the social realism of life
in a caravan park, but although the character of Bunny insists
'We could be on a tiny rock. Floating in space', Pearson knows
that grounding her fable in the here and now is necessary in

order for us to follow her on a magical journey, a journey where the arm of Jamie's Granny (the harbinger of death and peddler of suicide) can just drop off, and Bunny and George-Michael metamorphose into butterflies. However, none of this is as important as Pearson's less obvious achievement, which is to tell a story of such intense pain and loss, but in such an unflaggingly hilarious way, that we don't notice the hurt until it's too late.

Ramallah by David Greig was originally commissioned by the Royal Court Theatre, London, in a series of plays by playwrights who had had experience of teaching abroad. It was presented as a rehearsed reading in 2004 and received its first full production at the Tron Theatre, Glasgow, in May 2010 as part of a triple bill of work about Palestine called *From the West Bank*. The title is ironic because the play is set back home in Scotland and concerns, not the West Bank city, but how the returning traveller relates to his 'oriental' experience and, more precisely, how he may belong again back home – with an implicit question of where does the heart lie. *Ramallah* is in some ways a study for his full-length play *Damascus* (Traverse Theatre, 2007), in which a Scot nearly loses his heart on a brief visit to the Middle East.

Here the protagonist, Daniel, is a playwright who has been researching a play. It's a big risk for a playwright to write about a playwright, but, if it feels too self-referential from the pen of David Greig, it's worth noting that Daniel doesn't share Greig's sense of irony: he watched 'the kids on the waste ground throwing stones' without spotting the resonance of Palestinian youth rebelling against Israeli incursion. Greig testifies unapologetically to the unequal conflict in Palestine between the Palestinian people and the illegal Israeli settlers on their land. But there is a really interesting equation between Daniel's righteous anger about Zionist iniquities and Helen's implicit suggestion that Daniel – the interloper – should be more exercised by his own children than by the geopolitics of the Near East. Helen and their kids have had to conjure their own reduced family existence in Daniel's absence, and it's not been a bed of roses. *Ramallah* is the kind of micro-drama which both Scottish and English playwrights excel at: the shorter the play, the greater the importance attached to nuance. Here, even the act of smoking feels like an act of adultery.

If David Greig's *Ramallah* is a micro-drama, then *Harm* by Douglas Maxwell (Sweetscar at the Arches, Glasgow, 2006) must be a haiku. In this near-monologue for the father of a self-harming son, Maxwell demonstrates that it truly is possible to pack the story, the backstory, the complete world, even the offstage characters – and a huge heart – into seven minutes. It's a testament to that hoary old theatrical cliché 'less is more'; but then even that feels like too clinical an analysis of this body-blow of a play.

Better Days Better Knights by Stanley Eveling premiered at the Pool Lunch-Hour Theatre, Hanover Street, Edinburgh, in November 1971, and was revived at the King's Head, London, in 1976 in a production directed by Max Stafford-Clark. It is the oldest play in the volume but also, arguably, the most timeless: the waif-like Water Sprite Ondine proposes marriage to a decrepit Knight of the Realm (possibly the last of his kind) in order to render herself human. His dedication to the chivalric code forbids him to take advantage of her – whatever her watery charms – and, instead, he tries to bring her laughter, the human trait which has eluded her. When this fails, and a real live fire-breathing dragon appears (this almost certainly the last of its kind), the Knight's final act of chivalry is to sacrifice his imminent hard-earned retirement and slay the beast, propelling the Sprite into a cruel understanding of what being human is. Even within its brief thirty minutes, *Better Days Better Knights* luxuriates unashamedly in its own metaphor.

Stanley Eveling, who died on Christmas Eve 2008, fearlessly subtitled *Better Days Better Knights* 'a brief morality play', and, as Scotland's philosopher-playwright of the later twentieth century, he was well qualified to take the form of a medieval morality play, shoogle it around a bit with the form of a platonic dialogue (or as the critic Cordelia Oliver, in her review from December 1971 in *Plays & Players*, describes it, 'a dialogue of non-alignment'), and render the everyman characters not as archetypes, but as fully human – or at least striving to be. Eveling was always slightly ahead of his time: if the raggedy knight, nursing his mortal wound at the end of the play, feels Pythonesque in its absurdist humour, it's worth noting that he pre-dates the torso'ed Black Knight from *Monty Python and the Holy Grail* (1975) by four years.

It is a nice fact that there is a direct ancestral link between the old Pool Lunch-Hour programmes in Edinburgh in the last century and the A Play, a Pie and a Pint series in Glasgow in this one. In his *Scotsman* review of *Better Days Better Knights* (3 November 1971), the critic Allen Wright opined: 'This is the kind of entertainment which makes lunch-hour theatre worthwhile.' Eveling's playography is inextricably linked to the history (and philosophy) of the Traverse Theatre, primarily because his play *The Balachites* (1963) was the first new play by a living British playwright that the Traverse ever produced. It set a tone. His writing was deeply influenced by the great wave of European writing that the first incarnation of the Traverse (in Edinburgh's Lawnmarket) imported, uniquely, into British Theatre, much of it belonging to a French absurdist genre. Ultimately, however, Eveling was a great humanist. And to this end, *Better Days Better Knights* is a perfect epitaph.

Edinburgh
July 2010

Acknowledgements

Grateful thanks to Vicky Featherstone, David MacLennan and Joyce McMillan for illuminating and insightful conversations which could have gone on for ever; and especially to Katherine Mendelsohn at the Traverse Theatre for passing Stanley Eveling's forgotten gem to me. Thanks to Jamie, Drew and Lindsay for watering me while I read tens and tens of plays. And to David Greig, David Harrower, Nicola McCartney and Linda McLean: thank you for the fish supper.

Philip Howard

Philip was born and brought up in Yorkshire, read Classics at Girton College, Cambridge, and studied for a MLitt in Architectural History at the University of St Andrews.

He trained as a theatre director under Max Stafford-Clark at the Royal Court Theatre on the Regional Theatre Young Director Scheme from 1988–1990. He was Associate Director at the Traverse Theatre, Edinburgh, from 1993–1996 and Artistic Director from 1996–2007. Productions at the Traverse include twenty-four world premieres of plays by David Greig, David Harrower, Iain F MacLeod, Linda McLean, Henry Adam, Catherine Czerkawska, Catherine Grosvenor, Sue Glover, Iain Heggie, Jules Horne, Nicola McCartney, Ronan O'Donnell and the late Iain Crichton Smith. Awards include Fringe Firsts for the productions of *Kill the Old Torture Their Young*, *Wiping My Mother's Arse*, *Outlying Islands* (also Royal Court; World Stage Festival, Toronto) and *Damascus* (also Harbourfront Centre, Toronto; Off Broadway, New York; Meyerhold, Moscow; Tricycle, London; British Council tour to Near East and North Africa); Jury Special Award for Production of *Petrol Jesus Nightmare #5* (*In the Time of the Messiah*) at InFest, National Theatre of Priština, Kosovo. Other productions at the Traverse include *Faith Healer* by Brian Friel, *The Trestle at Pope Lick Creek* by Naomi Wallace, *Cuttin' a Rug* by John Byrne, *When the Bulbul Stopped Singing* by Raja Shehadeh (also Fadjr International Festival, Tehran; Off Broadway, New York; Amman, Jordan) and, as co-director, *Solemn Mass for a Full Moon in Summer* by Michel Tremblay (Traverse Theatre/Barbican). Productions elsewhere include *Fuenteovejuna* (Òran Mór, Glasgow), *Words of Advice for Young People* by Ioanna Anderson (Rough Magic, Dublin), *The Speculator* by David Greig in Catalan (Grec Festival, Barcelona/Edinburgh International Festival), *Entertaining Mr*

Sloane (Royal Theatre, Northampton) and *Something About Us* (Lyric Hammersmith Studio). Radio credits include *Being Norwegian* by David Greig, *The Gold Digger* by Iain F MacLeod (BBC Radio Scotland); *The Room* by Paul Brennen, *Life*: *an Audio Tour* by Jules Horne (BBC Radio 4).

Currently, Philip is teaching MLitt in Dramaturgy and Playwriting at University of Glasgow, Department of Theatre, Film and Television Studies; and working as a dramaturg for Calipo Theatre Company in Ireland. He is also the editor of *Scotland Plays* for Nick Hern Books (1997).

SNUFF

Davey Anderson

Davey Anderson comes from Glasgow. His work as playwright/director includes *Snuff* (Arches Theatre, as winner of the Arches Award for Stage Directors, runner up Meyer-Whitworth Award); *Rupture* (National Theatre of Scotland and Traverse Theatre) and *Blackout* (National Theatre New Connections). His other plays include *Wired* (Òran Mór, nominated Best Play, Critics' Awards for Theatre in Scotland); *Liar* (TAG Theatre Company and Sounds of Progress, Best Show for Children and Young People, Critics' Awards for Theatre in Scotland); *Clutter Keeps Company* (Birds of Paradise) and *Playback* (Ankur Theatre Productions).

Adaptations include *Zorro* (Visible Fictions and Traverse Theatre). Co-writing/directing credits include *Mixter Maxter* (National Theatre of Scotland and St Magnus Festival, Orkney). Other directing credits include *Rocketville* (Òran Mór). As Associate Director: *Home* (National Theatre of Scotland) and *Architecting* (The TEAM and National Theatre of Scotland). His work as musical director/composer includes *Peter Pan* (National Theatre of Scotland and Barbican), *Be Near Me* (National Theatre of Scotland and Donmar Warehouse); *Oresteia* (Lazzi Experimental Arts Unit & Cumbernauld Theatre) and *Black Watch* (National Theatre of Scotland, nominated Best Use of Music, Critics' Awards for Theatre in Scotland). He was Director-in-Residence with the National Theatre of Scotland 2006–07 and will be an Associate Playwright with the Playwrights' Studio Scotland 2010–11.

Snuff was first performed at the Arches Theatre, Glasgow, on 5 April 2005, with the following cast:

KEVIN	Brian Ferguson
PAMELA	Siobhan Reilly
BILLY	Steven Ritchie

Director	Davey Anderson
Designer	Will Holt
Lighting and	
Sound Designer	Graham Sutherland
Photographer and	
Projections	Clementine Sandison

The production then transferred to the Traverse Theatre, Edinburgh for the Festival Fringe 2005, and toured the UK in 2006 in a co-production with the National Theatre of Scotland.

Characters

KEVIN

PAMELA

BILLY

A small room in a high-rise flat. There's a door on one side leading out to the communal close. On the other side is a corridor leading in towards the kitchen. A window faces out onto an urban wasteland. Noises seep through the walls from the world beyond.

The room is cluttered with cardboard boxes, tabloid newspapers and magazines. A television set and video player sit on top of a small filing cabinet. On the floor nearby there's a pile of video-tapes, each one labelled with a different name.

KEVIN *enters from the kitchen carrying an unmarked video and scans the room looking for something. He rummages through drawers and boxes until he finds it: his marker pen. He writes the name 'PAMELA' on the label, puts the tape in the machine and presses play.*

The image flickers to life on the television screen. The video is halfway through. KEVIN *watches himself on video interviewing his sister.*

KEVIN *(on screen)*. Fucking sit doon.

PAMELA *(on screen)*. Don't touch me.

KEVIN *(on screen)*. Where did ye get they claes?

PAMELA *(on screen)*. They're mine.

KEVIN *(on screen)*. Where d'ye get them?

PAMELA *(on screen)*. I bought them.

KEVIN *(on screen)*. Did ye?

PAMELA *(on screen)*. Yeh.

KEVIN *(on screen)*. Ye bought these?

PAMELA *(on screen)*. Aye.

KEVIN *(on screen)*. Where?

PAMELA (*on screen*). In the fucking shops, ya dafty.

KEVIN (*on screen*). Don't talk tae me like that.

PAMELA (*on screen*). Leave me alone.

KEVIN (*on screen*). How did ye buy this? Ye don't have any money.

PAMELA (*on screen*). I didnae steal it, right?

KEVIN (*on screen*). Where did ye get it then?

PAMELA (*on screen*). It wis a present.

KEVIN (*on screen*). Oh aye, who gave it tae ye?

PAMELA (*on screen*). Stop it, Kevin, that hurts!

KEVIN (*on screen*). It's meant tae hurt.

PAMELA (*on screen*). This isnae funny. I don't want tae play any more.

KEVIN (*on screen*). This isnae a game, Pamela.

PAMELA (*on screen*). Whit d'ye want?

KEVIN (*on screen*). You know whit I want.

PAMELA (*on screen*). I could get you done for this. Child abuse.

KEVIN (*on screen*). Where did ye get the claes?

PAMELA (*on screen*). Fuck off.

KEVIN (*on screen*). Just tell me.

PAMELA (*on screen*). You cannae dae this tae me.

KEVIN (*on screen*). Where did ye get them?

PAMELA (*on screen*). I could get you killed.

   Pause.

KEVIN (*on screen*). Whit? Whit did you jist say?

PAMELA (*on screen*). You heard.

KEVIN (*on screen*). Is that a threat? Get Mohammed tae break ma legs?

PAMELA (*on screen*). I can get you done over. I'll tell Billy whit you've done tae me.

KEVIN (*on screen*). Whit? You'll tell who?

PAMELA (*on screen*). I can get you tae disappear.

KEVIN (*on screen*). You'll get who? Whit ye talking aboot? Billy's no even here.

PAMELA (*on screen*). I'll get you hit so hard ye fucking break.

KEVIN (*on screen*). Billy's away, ya stupid cunt.

PAMELA (*on screen*). Is he?

KEVIN (*on screen*). He's been away two year. You're fucking tripping.

PAMELA (*on screen*). Whit dae you know?

KEVIN (*on screen*). Fucking sit doon.

PAMELA (*on screen*). Don't touch me.

Suddenly, there's a knock at the door. KEVIN *turns off the video. He listens. There's another knock.*

KEVIN. Hullo?

BILLY (*off*). Hullo?

KEVIN. Hullo?

BILLY (*off*). Hullo?

KEVIN. Whit d'ye want?

BILLY (*off*). Kev, is that you?

KEVIN. Who's that?

BILLY (*off*). It's me. Open the door.

KEVIN. Who is it?

BILLY (*off*). It's me, Billy.

KEVIN. Billy who?

BILLY (*off*). King Billy of the fucking Boyne, who d'ye think? Open the door.

KEVIN. Wait a minute.

KEVIN *hides the pile of videos on a high shelf.*

BILLY (*off*). Whit ye daeing in there?

KEVIN. I'm coming.

BILLY (*off*). Can ye hear me?

KEVIN. I says I'm coming.

He goes to the door and unlocks it.

BILLY. Kev, hurry up and open the door.

KEVIN. Alright, for fuck's sake. Calm the beans.

He slowly opens the door, concealing himself. BILLY peers into the room.

BILLY. Hullo? Knock, knock, anybody home? You there, Kev? Whit ye up tae?

KEVIN *slams shut the door and jumps on* BILLY.

KEVIN. Attack!

BILLY. Get aff me, ya poofter.

KEVIN. Surrender!

BILLY. Get aff.

KEVIN. D'ye surrender?

BILLY. Dae I fuck.

KEVIN. That's right, mate, never surrender.

BILLY. Weakling like you, I could take you any day.

KEVIN. Ye think so?

BILLY. I know I could.

KEVIN. Take me where, up the arsehole?

BILLY. In yer dreams.

KEVIN. Come ahead.

BILLY. I'll stick ma foot up yer arsehole.

KEVIN. Yes please.

BILLY. Put it away, Kev, I'm no in the mood.

KEVIN. Don't have whit it takes?

BILLY. You wouldnae know what hit ye.

KEVIN. I bet ye say that tae all the boys.

> KEVIN *turns on the main light in the room.* BILLY *looks around.*

BILLY. Fuck's sake! Whit's happened in here?

KEVIN. Nothing.

BILLY. It's a fucking tip. Looks like a bomb's hit it.

KEVIN. Whit are you, ma fucking maw?

> BILLY *tries to push a heavy box.*

BILLY. Whit ye got in here? Dead bodies?

KEVIN. Jist stuff.

> BILLY *looks at a massive pile of magazines.*

BILLY. Whit's this?

KEVIN. Put it back.

BILLY. How?

KEVIN. You're messing up ma system.

BILLY. Whit?

KEVIN. I know exactly where everything is.

BILLY. Aye, right.

KEVIN. It's all categorised and compartmentalised and clearly labelled for ease of access.

BILLY. You taking the piss?

KEVIN. But I'm the only wan that understands the filing system, eh? Means naebody stumbles across anything they shouldnae.

BILLY. Like whit?

KEVIN. Things they shouldnae see.

BILLY *looks at* KEVIN *and laughs*.

Whit you fucking laughing at?

BILLY. Check the state ae ye.

KEVIN. Whit?

BILLY. Fucking look at ye.

KEVIN. Whit ye saying?

BILLY. Nothing. But, fuck's sake…

KEVIN. Whit?

BILLY. Whit ye daeing wearing a suit?

KEVIN. This? It's ma uniform.

BILLY. Eh? Whit uniform?

KEVIN. Ma uniform of respectability, that's whit.

BILLY. Shut up.

KEVIN. I'm telling ye.

BILLY. Whit happened tae the skinhead? You used tae be wan of the boot boys.

KEVIN. Least I don't look like a fucking ned.

BILLY. Since when d'you know about fashion?

KEVIN. I know that you look like a prick.

BILLY. Shut it, ya fanny.

KEVIN. D'you walk up here in those trainers?

BILLY. Aye, so?

KEVIN. You need tae watch yersel, wearing them.

BILLY. How?

KEVIN. Some cunt will have them off ye.

BILLY. Will they fuck.

KEVIN. They're too shiny, new and white. Ye need tae scruff them up a bit. Here, I'll christen them for ye.

BILLY. Fuck off.

KEVIN. They need broken in.

BILLY. I'll fucking break you in. I'll fucking christen you. Beat it, ya dick. I'll fucking get you back.

KEVIN. Ooooh, I'm scared. Whit ye gonnae dae? Suffocate me wae yer shell suit?

BILLY. I'll take that belt aff ye and scelp ye across the heed wae it, ya trumpet.

KEVIN. Naw, man, then ma troosers'll fall doon and ye'll see ma tadger.

BILLY. Ye know whit ye look like, Kev? Ye look like a clown. All ye need's the red nose and the big curly wig.

KEVIN. Naw, a blue nose.

BILLY. D'ye dae any tricks?

KEVIN. Aye. Here's a good wan. Look whit's up ma sleeve.

BILLY *looks*. KEVIN *slaps him*.

BILLY. Very funny.

KEVIN. Ye never saw that wan coming, did ye? D'ye no learn how tae defend yersel when ye were away? D'ye no learn tae prepare for a surprise attack?

BILLY. Wis that an attack? Oh, sorry, I thought ye were jist trying tae feel me up.

KEVIN. Don't worry, Billy, there's plenty more where that came fae.

BILLY. Oh aye?

KEVIN. Aye, I've got a few more tricks up ma sleeve.

BILLY. That right?

KEVIN. Jist you wait.

Pause.

BILLY. So where's yer lovely assistant?

KEVIN. Eh?

BILLY. Where's yer sister?

KEVIN. Whit, Pamela?

BILLY. You've only got wan sister.

KEVIN. Don't remind me. (*Beat.*) Whit makes ye think she'll be here?

BILLY. She lives here.

KEVIN. So?

BILLY. Is she no in?

KEVIN. Naw, Pamela's dead.

BILLY. Shut it, Kev.

KEVIN. She might be.

BILLY. She's no.

KEVIN. How dae you know?

BILLY *smiles and looks around the room.*

BILLY. It's funny.

KEVIN. Whit's funny?

BILLY. It looks different, this place, eh? But nothing's really changed.

Pause.

KEVIN. Why are you so interested in ma sister?

BILLY *shrugs.* KEVIN *shrugs back at him. A car passes in the street below with music blaring.*

D'ye want a cup of tea?

BILLY. Aye, alright.

KEVIN. Milk and two?

BILLY. No milk. I've started taking it black.

KEVIN. Funny that, eh?

BILLY. Whit?

KEVIN. How people change. (*Beat*.) Wait here.

BILLY. I'll come and keep ye company.

KEVIN. It's alright.

BILLY. I don't mind.

KEVIN. The kitchen's a mess.

BILLY. So?

KEVIN. It smells, ye know? I wouldnae go in there if I wis you.

BILLY. You trying hide something, Kev?

KEVIN. Aye, I've got six deid bodies laid out on the floor. In a pyramid. No a pretty sight. I'm jist waiting for the right time tae take them doon tae the incinerator. Heavy fuckers, though. I might need tae chop them up.

BILLY. Well, gies a shout if ye need a hand, eh?

KEVIN. Aye, I'll let ye know.

KEVIN *exits to the kitchen.* BILLY *watches him go then starts to look around the room. He notices the videos on the high shelf.*

BILLY. Here, Kev, d'ye remember that wee darkie that used tae live up the top floor? Used tae fucking chase us doon the stair cos we'd wind him up, eh? Put dog shite through his letter box and all that. Then he'd come oot and try and gies a doing. Remember?

I went intae school wan day and says tae the teacher, how come he looks different fae us? And she says, that's cos his mammy wis bad and this is God's punishment. She couldnae keep her legs shut. She fucked a black guy. Then he fucked off. And she wis left wae this wee darkie kid.

So I says tae you, mon up and we'll try and get intae his house. So we went upstairs wae a copy of Sonic and knocked the door. Thought he might kick fuck oot ae us. But he didnae. He took us inside and let us have a go of his Mega Drive.

Then I thought it would be funny if we gied him a wee fright, ye know? Jist tae wind him up. So we grabbed him and dangled him oot the windae. Pretended we were gonnae let him fall. That wis a laugh. But his maw came in and gied us a leathering. Remember that? Never went back up there again. Stayed well away fae him after that.

KEVIN *re-enters, unseen, carrying two mugs.*

Whit wis his name again? D'ye ever hear whit happened tae him?

KEVIN. Here's yer tea.

BILLY *jumps.*

BILLY. That wis quick.

KEVIN. Aye, well, the kettle wis already boiled. (*Beat.*) Who were ye talking aboot?

BILLY. Disnae matter.

KEVIN *hands one of the mugs to* BILLY.

KEVIN. This wan's yours.

BILLY. D'ye put milk in it?

KEVIN. Aye, sorry. My hand slipped. I'll make ye a new wan if ye want.

BILLY. Naw, naw, don't be daft. This is fine.

KEVIN. Ye sure?

BILLY. Aye.

KEVIN. Jist as well. There's nae mair tea bags. (*Beat.*) Well?

BILLY. Well whit?

KEVIN. Have a seat.

BILLY. D'you no want a seat?

KEVIN. There's only wan chair.

BILLY. I don't mind the floor.

KEVIN. Fucking sit doon. (*Beat*.) I'll need tae get some mair.

BILLY. Whit, chairs?

KEVIN. Tea. I'll need tae get some mair tea.

They drink their tea. BILLY *looks at the boxes.*

BILLY. You still no unpacked yet?

KEVIN. Naw.

BILLY. Ye should get yersel settled in a bit.

KEVIN. I'm moving oot soon.

BILLY. Where ye gon?

KEVIN. Somewhere else.

BILLY. Funny that. Somewhere nice?

KEVIN. Might be.

BILLY *looks at the door.*

BILLY. Fuck's sake. How many locks ye got on that door?

KEVIN. Well, ye cannae be too careful.

BILLY. Think somebody's gonnae break in?

KEVIN. It's happened before.

BILLY. That right?

KEVIN. Aye.

BILLY. Steal anything?

KEVIN. Don't know.

BILLY. Whit d'ye mean, ye don't know?

KEVIN. No here.

BILLY. Eh?

KEVIN. It wis doonstair. Kicked the door in. Knocked the folk aboot a bit. Don't know if they took anything. Whacked them wae a golf club. Fucking hospital job.

BILLY. Who's this?

KEVIN. Folk doonstair. Smashed the place up. Wrote a message on the wall. Jist two words, in big fuck-off letters.

BILLY. Whit d'they write?

KEVIN. Go home.

BILLY. Go home?

KEVIN. Aye.

BILLY. Is that it?

KEVIN. Aye.

Pause.

Did I tell ye I got a new job?

BILLY. Naw. Where abouts?

KEVIN. In the bookies. Started a few month ago.

BILLY. Whit's that like?

KEVIN. It's alright.

BILLY. Had yer fingers in the till yet?

KEVIN. Naw.

BILLY. Bet ye have. Whit's the odds? I bet ye a tenner ye get the sack.

KEVIN. No chance.

BILLY. I bet ye.

KEVIN. Nut.

BILLY. Bet ye.

KEVIN. Nut.

BILLY. Bet ye!

KEVIN. Nut.

BILLY. Bastard. (*Beat*.) So whit time d'ye start?

KEVIN. Half past.

BILLY. You're late.

KEVIN. No the day. It's ma day aff.

BILLY. Lucky you.

KEVIN. Naw, lucky you.

Pause.

BILLY. I'll jist take these mugs back tae the kitchen, eh?

KEVIN. I hate ma job. I'm gonnae sack it in. All the auld men coming in, throwing away their pensions. And for whit? A buzz? A few seconds of pleasure. It never lasts. They always lose. And it's no jist their money they're pissing away. It's their dignity. Their pride. It's criminal whit we dae to those auld men. They're all war heroes and that. Or they would be, given half the chance. They made this country whit it is today. And how dae we repay them? By stealing their hard-earned cash. No respect. Kids these days don't know whit it's like tae suffer.

KEVIN *looks at* BILLY.

How long've you been here?

BILLY. Eh? I jist got here.

KEVIN. I mean, how long ye been back?

BILLY. Back home? Well. Jist. No long.

KEVIN. How long?

BILLY. A couple of days, ye know?

KEVIN. A couple of days?

BILLY. Aye, jist a few days.

KEVIN. A few days?

BILLY. Mibbae a week.

KEVIN. A week?

BILLY. Aye.

KEVIN. You've been back a week?

BILLY. Aye.

KEVIN. A whole week? (*Beat*.) Ye been busy?

BILLY. Aye, quite busy. Whit aboot you?

KEVIN. Oh, ye know me, never an idle moment. No enough hours in the day. (*Beat*.) You seen anybody? Any of the boys?

BILLY. Naw.

KEVIN. Whit ye been daeing?

BILLY. Resting.

KEVIN. Keeping a low profile?

BILLY. Aye, something like that.

KEVIN. A whole week. (*Beat*.) Anybody would think you've been avoiding me.

BILLY. Eh?

KEVIN. I'm no saying ye have. I'm jist saying it might look that way tae other people.

BILLY. Whit other people?

KEVIN. Anybody looking at the situation objectively, ye know? Withoot knowing the full details of the individual subjectivities.

BILLY. Whit ye talking aboot?

KEVIN. Any outside observer, no familiar wae the intricacies of oor relationship, might mistake your behaviour as being a wee bit odd.

BILLY. You gon daft?

KEVIN. I'm no saying it is, mind, I'm jist hypothesising aboot how it might appear, ye know, tae a stranger. Why it's taken you so long tae come up and see yer mate, yer best pal,

Kevin. Might seem a bit odd, that, tae some people. I mean, a whole week.

BILLY. You're the wan that's fucking odd.

KEVIN. Course, the thing aboot being auld friends, is that we know things aboot each other that strangers cannae see. Cos we've got a history. Means we understaun each other, like, intuitively. Don't ye think?

BILLY. Dae we fuck.

KEVIN. Like, I get the impression there's a reason you came up here that ye don't want tae tell me. That there's something ye don't want tae talk aboot. Am I right? And I get the feeling that you know that I know that you know there's no point lying tae me. Cos I can see right through ye like a glass tumbler. And I can fucking tell when you're talking pish. Know whit I mean?

Pause.

BILLY. Is this supposed tae be some kind of interrogation?

KEVIN. Jist passing the time of day.

KEVIN *opens a drawer of the filing cabinet, brings out a Polaroid camera and takes* BILLY*'s picture.*

BILLY. Whit's that for?

KEVIN. Reference.

He writes BILLY*'s name on the photograph, then pins it to the wall and watches the image develop.*

BILLY. Whit's on the videos, Kev?

KEVIN. What videos?

BILLY. All these videotapes. Whit's on them?

KEVIN. That's private, Billy.

BILLY. Whit is it, a wee bit of home-made entertainment?

KEVIN. It's jist a project I'm working on.

BILLY. Oh aye? Can I see?

KEVIN. Naw.

BILLY. How no?

KEVIN. Nobody's allowed tae see whit's on those tapes except me. Like I says, it's private.

BILLY. Are ye still working on it, is that it?

KEVIN. Aye, it's no finished yet.

BILLY. Can I see it when it's finished?

KEVIN. It's no finished.

BILLY. But see, when it is finished, can I see it then?

KEVIN. Aye. Once it's finished.

BILLY. When will it be finished?

KEVIN. I jist need wan mair subject. Jist one more and then it's done.

Pause.

Ye want tae know something, Billy? See since you left, this place has gone tae the dogs. Swear tae God. All the decent folk moved oot. Got transferred doon tae the new flats by the river. Most of the flats were empty. So they started boarding up all the windaes and the doors. The only people left were the junkies, the hardnuts, the perverts and the freaks. Turned intae a mad hoose, this place. A big, damp, concrete, mental asylum.

The coonsil telt us they were gonnae level this block, ye know? Blow it up. They gave us six month. They says, as soon as we find ye somewhere else tae live, we're gonnae demolish the flats. So we waited. Nothing happened. Six month passed, still nothing. And I thought, well, this is it. They're jist gonnae demolish the flats, junkies and all. Bury us alive in a mountain of ash and rubble.

I wis quite looking forward tae it, tae be honest. Jist kind of resigned myself tae the fact, ye know? Jist got used the idea of inevitable doom.

Then wan morning this truck pulls up doonstair. These guys come oot and start unloading. Furniture. Fucking sofas and tables and beds and that. Loads of them. I wis like that, oh aye, whit's this all aboot? And they start taking all this stuff intae the empty flats. Opening the doors, fixing the windaes, getting them ready. I says tae wan of the guys, whit's gon on? He's like that, oh we're jist moving the furniture. I says, aye, but who's it for? I dinnae ken, that's nane of ma business, I jist get paid tae shift the furniture.

And see when they arrive, it's the middle of the night. These two coaches drive up tae the flats. I hear the engines. It wakes me up. I goes tae the windae, looks doon. I cannae see too well. The street light's flickering. But something fucking weird is going on. All these people are getting bundled aff the buses, wae carrier bags and that.

And they're all stauning there. And no a single wan ae them has a white face. I'm like that, fuck me.

I sprint doon the stair. The whole car park's swarming wae fucking foreigners. Where's the driver? Naebody's listening. Where's the fucking driver? Some of them look at me but naebody speaks. Fuck's sake, dae nane of yous cunts speak any fucking English?

Then they all start piling in the door. Up the lift and up the stairwell. Stopping off at every flaer tae fill up their new luxury apartments. I'm trying tae block the entrance, but there's too many of them.

Why the fuck does somebody else no wake up and see whit's going on?

If only Billy wis here, I thought, he would help me. He'd be doon here in a flash. We could take them on, jist the two of us. Dae a bit of kung fu and whip all of their black asses. We'd drive them oot before they could say Osama bin Laden. We'd fucking show them.

But you wurnae here. You were away. And it wis jist me. I couldnae stop them on ma ain.

Next thing ye know, all the doors slam shut, the buses drive off. Silence. I'm left stauning there in the pissing rain. Freezing my bollocks off. No a fucking thing I can dae aboot it. I shouts up at the flats, naebody telt me!

That's the worst of it. It all jist happened like that. Naebody fucking telt me.

Pause.

BILLY. Kev, it's like I says, it looks different, this place, but it's jist the same. Nothing's changed.

KEVIN. Everything's changed.

BILLY. It's jist different folk wae the same shitty problems.

KEVIN. Naw, it's no jist different folk. The thing is, Billy, these people are different. And the problems are deep. They're in the floor. In the walls. Can ye no feel it?

BILLY. Feel whit?

KEVIN. They're surrounding us. Everywhere ye look. They're stealing our air.

BILLY. You're paranoid, Kev.

KEVIN. Shhhh!

BILLY. Whit?

KEVIN. Shhhh!

KEVIN *writes on the wall, 'They're listening.'*

BILLY *takes the pen and writes, 'Who?'*

KEVIN *replies, 'Them.'*

BILLY *moves to a different wall and writes, 'Fuck off.'*

Silently, KEVIN *stands on the chair and presses his ear to the wall.* BILLY *watches.* KEVIN *listens for a while then offers the chair to* BILLY. BILLY *steps up and presses his ear to the wall.* KEVIN *locks the door then goes to the window.* BILLY *looks at* KEVIN.

BILLY. You're off yer fucking nut.

KEVIN *looks out of the window.*

Seriously, man, you need psychiatric attention. (*Beat.*) Whit ye daeing noo?

KEVIN. Ye see that white van doon there? It's been parked there for three days. It's no moved wance. It's jist sitting there, underneath ma windae. (*Beat.*) Ye cannae see it, Billy, but they've got intae the walls.

BILLY. I cannae see anything.

KEVIN *locks the door.*

KEVIN. D'ye want tae dae something for me?

BILLY. Whit?

KEVIN. See that videotape that's in the machine?

BILLY. Aye?

KEVIN. D'ye want tae rewind it tae the beginning for me?

Reluctantly, BILLY *presses the rewind button.*

I've got something tae show ye.

BILLY. Whit?

KEVIN *goes to the filing cabinet.*

KEVIN. Wait till ye see this.

He takes out a handgun and points it at BILLY.

BILLY. Whit's that?

KEVIN. Whit d'ye think it is, soldier boy? It's a gun. You should know aboot these things.

BILLY. Sure it's no a toy?

KEVIN. Only wan way tae find out.

BILLY. Can I've a look?

KEVIN. Aye, here ye go.

BILLY. Nice machine. Got any bullets?

KEVIN. Naw.

BILLY. So why ye showing me?

KEVIN. Jist want tae know whit ye think. Is it any good?

BILLY. Depends. Depends whit you're gonnae use it for.

KEVIN. D'ye ever dream aboot shooting somebody?

BILLY. Aye, all the time.

KEVIN. I don't mean Iraqis, Billy. I mean, if ye could shoot anybody. Who would ye shoot, if ye could shoot anybody in the world?

BILLY. Ye mean, apart fae you?

KEVIN. Aye, anybody apart fae me.

BILLY. I don't know.

KEVIN. Anybody.

BILLY. I cannae think of anybody.

KEVIN. Ye know your problem, Billy? Ye've got no imagination.

BILLY. Whit's that supposed tae mean?

KEVIN. Jist give us the gun back, eh?

BILLY. Naw. Whit the fuck ye talking aboot?

KEVIN. Gies the gun.

BILLY. You trying tae say yer better than me?

KEVIN. I didnae say that.

BILLY. Using all they big words and that, trying tae make me look stupit.

KEVIN. Shut up.

BILLY. I'm no as daft as ye think, Kev.

KEVIN. I didnae say ye were daft.

BILLY. I've got a few tricks up ma sleeve as well.

KEVIN. Gonnae gie me it?

BILLY. Ye shouldnae have got it oot in the first place.

KEVIN *packs the gun away.*

KEVIN. Right, well, d'ye want another cup of tea?

BILLY. Thought ye'd ran oot.

KEVIN. I forgot. (*Beat.*) I'm away for a slash.

KEVIN *exits in the direction of the kitchen.* BILLY *waits until he's gone then presses play on the video player. The image of* PAMELA *comes up on the screen. The tape is at the beginning. Their conversation starts:*

PAMELA (*on screen*). So whit dae I need tae do?

KEVIN (*on screen*). Jist talk.

PAMELA (*on screen*). Jist talk? Is that it? Is this like wan of they video diaries, like in *Big Brother*?

KEVIN (*on screen*). Naw.

PAMELA (*on screen*). Aye, like in the diary room. It's day one in the Big Brother house. Pamela is called into the diary room. I nominate Kevin for eviction. Get it? Big brother. That's you.

KEVIN (*on screen*). Aye, very good, noo gonnae stop fucking about.

PAMELA (*on screen*). Fuck's sake, I'm only joking. Right, so whit d'ye want me tae talk aboot?

KEVIN (*on screen*). Talk aboot here.

PAMELA (*on screen*). Whit? Where I live? Aye, well I can tell ye all aboot that cos I know every cunt roon here. Aye, fucking hunners of pals. I like everybody, me. And I'm dead popular cos I'm easy to talk tae and that.

KEVIN (*on screen*). Aye, right.

PAMELA (*on screen*). I'm a good listener. Sal says I've got a nice personality and that's more important than anything. It disnae matter where ye are and whit ye dae, as long as you're happy.

KEVIN (*on screen*). And are ye happy?

PAMELA (*on screen*). I'm always happy.

KEVIN (*on screen*). Are ye happy, Pamela?

PAMELA (*on screen*). Don't start, Kevin. (*Beat.*) I fucking hate it here, it's a shithole. I want tae move somewhere else, ye know? Go somewhere.

KEVIN (*on screen*). Where?

PAMELA (*on screen*). Anywhere. Fucking Spain. Disnae matter. Jist somewhere else.

KEVIN (*on screen*). Whit dae you know aboot Spain?

PAMELA (*on screen*). I went tae Spain wance wae ma pals. Clubbing and all that. It wis a pure laugh. I tried tae get a tan, but I jist got burnt. And see Kelly-Anne, she got a fucking tattoo on her arse cheek. I says tae her, whit's the point of that, naebody's gonnae see it. She says, aye, if I wear a G-string. And I can still cover it up for work, know whit I mean?

Fuck, I never told ye aboot Kelly-Anne. She's fucking pregnant. She's asked me tae be the godmother. I wis like that, pure greeting and all that. I love kids.

The live KEVIN *re-enters and stands in the doorway. He watches* BILLY *watching the video, without making a sound.*

KEVIN (*on screen*). Have you got a boyfriend?

PAMELA (*on screen*). Whit?

KEVIN (*on screen*). Have ye got a boyfriend, Pamela?

PAMELA (*on screen*). Right, that's enough, Kevin, turn it off.

The live KEVIN *suddenly interrupts.*

KEVIN. What the fuck d'ye think you're daeing?

BILLY. Nothing.

BILLY turns off the video.

KEVIN. I thought I told you no tae touch anything.

BILLY. I know, but…

KEVIN. Whit? D'ye think I wis only joking? Thought I wis clowning about?

BILLY. It's no like that.

KEVIN. Naw?

BILLY. Naw.

KEVIN. What's it like then?

BILLY. I jist wanted tae see.

KEVIN. And whit did ye see?

BILLY. Nothing.

Pause.

KEVIN. I'm gonnae put a proposition tae you, Billy. And I don't expect ye tae answer right away. I'll give ye time tae formulate yer response. But I'm beginning tae suspect that you didnae come up here tae see me. I'm starting tae think that you wurnae expecting me tae be here at all. That the true nature and purpose of your visit wis tae sneak intae ma home and consort wae ma wee sister. Noo, tell me I'm wrong. Go on, tell me I'm wrong.

BILLY. It's no whit ye think, Kev.

KEVIN. Naw?

BILLY. Naw. I saw Pamela the other day. She asked me up here. I didnae know if I should come. I didnae even know if you still lived here, eh? (*Beat.*) She says she wis in some kind of trouble. I don't know whit. She wanted tae speak tae me. (*Beat.*) I think she wis probably winding me up.

KEVIN. Sounds like it, Billy. Sounds like she wis yanking your chain.

BILLY. She's made me look like a right fanny. I mean, she's no even here. Is she?

KEVIN. Naw. She's no even here.

Pause.

BILLY. Is she here?

KEVIN. Naw. I think she wis playing games wae ye. (*Beat.*) Mind you, she could still turn up. I mean, she might walk through that door at any moment. That would be a laugh, eh, if she walked in the noo?

BILLY. Aye, that would be funny.

KEVIN. She'd take wan look at your face and pish herself laughing.

BILLY. Aye, that would be fucking hilarious.

KEVIN. Tell ye whit, why don't ye put it back on?

BILLY. Whit?

KEVIN. The video. Press play and I'll watch it wae ye.

BILLY *reluctantly pushes the play button. The video springs back into life.*

(*On screen.*) Where are we now?

PAMELA (*on screen*). Go away.

KEVIN (*on screen*). For the camera.

PAMELA (*on screen*). We're in my bedroom.

KEVIN (*on screen*). Good. (*Beat.*) Tell me something aboot yersel.

PAMELA (*on screen*). Like whit?

KEVIN (*on screen*). Something I don't already know. (*Beat.*) Whit dae ye like?

PAMELA (*on screen*). I don't know.

KEVIN (*on screen*). Anything.

PAMELA (*on screen*). I hate that thing in ma face all the time.

KEVIN (*on screen*). How dae ye?

PAMELA (*on screen*). I'm trying tae go out.

KEVIN (*on screen*). Come on. Ye were singing earlier on. Dae ye like singing?

PAMELA (*on screen*). It's alright.

KEVIN (*on screen*). Dae ye want tae be a singer?

PAMELA (*on screen*). Mibbae?

KEVIN (*on screen*). Where are ye going?

PAMELA (*on screen*). I'm going out.

KEVIN (*on screen*). Who would ye vote for, Tories or Labour?

PAMELA (*on screen*). Eh?

KEVIN (*on screen*). If ye had tae vote, who would ye vote for, Tories or Labour?

PAMELA (*on screen*). None of them.

KEVIN (*on screen*). Look, Pamela, somebody's got a gun tae yer head, who are ye voting for?

PAMELA (*on screen*). Whit's that wan? Kilroy. He's alright.

KEVIN (*on screen*). Right. God. Dae ye believe in him?

PAMELA (*on screen*). Aye.

KEVIN (*on screen*). Which God?

PAMELA (*on screen*). Eh?

KEVIN (*on screen*). Which God?

PAMELA (*on screen*). Whit is this, anyway? Oh I get it, is this like in that movie? Whit's it called? The wan aboot the guy who watches videos of people talking cos he cannae get it up. Is that like you, Kev, is that how ye need tae make these videos?

KEVIN (*on screen*). Ye never answered the fucking question.

The live KEVIN *stops the video and stands in front of the TV.*

See, it's jist a video. People talking. Nothing special.

KEVIN *ejects the videotape.*

BILLY. Kev?

KEVIN. Whit?

BILLY. Kev?

KEVIN. Whit?

BILLY. Ye know how ye were saying ye jist need wan mair?

KEVIN. Aye?

BILLY. Well, I'll dae wan for ye, if ye want.

KEVIN. You want tae dae a video?

BILLY. Jist tae help ye out, ye know? So's it's finished. I'll be the last wan, right?

KEVIN. Aye.

BILLY. And then it's done.

KEVIN. Ye willnae fuck about?

BILLY. Naw.

KEVIN. Cos it disnae work if ye fuck about.

BILLY. I willnae fuck about.

KEVIN. Then say ye want tae dae it.

BILLY. I want tae dae it.

KEVIN. Say it like ye mean it.

BILLY. I really want tae dae it. I want tae make a video.

KEVIN *gets out the video camera and sets it up. He rummages through the biggest box.*

KEVIN. Right, whit costume d'ye want, Billy? Military dictator or guerrilla rebel? Naw, I know. I know jist the thing for you.

He takes out an orange boiler suit.

Illegal combatant.

BILLY. Whit the fuck's this?

KEVIN. We'll get tae that later.

He throws the 'costume' onto the floor.

Gonnae gies a hand a minute?

BILLY. Whit?

KEVIN. Jist gies a hand tae put this on the wall, eh?

    BILLY *helps* KEVIN *pin up an enormous Union Jack flag.*

BILLY. Fucking hell. Where d'ye get this stuff?

KEVIN. Never mind that. (*Beat.*) Right, are ye ready?

BILLY. Aye.

    KEVIN *switches the camera to record.*

KEVIN. On ye go.

BILLY. Whit d'ye want me tae talk aboot?

KEVIN. Where are we?

BILLY. We're in a room, in a flat, in a tower block. But it's pure stinking, man. See the guy that lives here, Kev, he's a total jakey.

KEVIN. And where's he?

BILLY. Behind the camera. Get it right up ye.

KEVIN. Very funny. Noo, whit country are we in?

BILLY. The United Kingdom.

KEVIN. Of whit?

BILLY. Great Britain and Northern Ireland.

KEVIN. Whit's the first two lines of the national anthem?

BILLY. God save oor gracious Queen. (*Beat.*) I cannae mind how it goes after that.

KEVIN. Whit's wrong wae you?

BILLY. Nothing.

    Pause.

I've been having these dreams. Nightmares. Every night the same dream. I'm in this place, right? It's kind of like here. I mean, it is here. But it's there as well, ye know? It's weird.

We're driving past the flats. I'm in the wagon wae the platoon. Everybody's sitting in the back, having a laugh.

Next thing, the wagon stops and we all nearly fall oot. Whit the fuck's going on? Whit have we stopped for?

Then we see her, stauning in front of us. Right in the middle of the road. It's a woman. A young woman. But we cannae see her face cos she's got it covered up. Her whole body is covered up wae wan of they things ye get in Afghanistan. Whit d'ye call them? A burqa. Something like that. Bright blue. Glimmering. We're all like that, staring at her. Hypnotised. And she's jist stauning there, totally still. Naebody moves.

She's got a bomb, that's whit everybody's thinking. She's gonnae blow us all tae fuck. I'm sweating, hardly breathing. I stand up and point ma gun at her. Don't fucking move! Dae exactly whit I tell ye! My finger's trembling over the trigger. Take off the burqa! She disnae move. Take it off or I'll fucking shoot ye! She still disnae move. I'm starting tae squeeze the trigger. Hands shaking. Take it off now!

Then suddenly she moves. She reaches doon tae lift the fabric. And she throws it over her heid.

So she's stauning there, completely naked. Nothing on. Nae bombs. Nothing. I feel dizzy. Cos she's looking at me. I mean, mibbae she's looking at all of us, but it feels like she's looking right at me. And I know her. I recognise her. It's Pamela.

KEVIN. D'you jist make that up?

BILLY. Naw, it wis a dream.

KEVIN. Funny dream that. (*Beat.*) Right, put on the costume.

KEVIN *throws* BILLY *the orange boiler suit.* BILLY *looks at it for a second, then puts it on. Meanwhile,* KEVIN *reaches into the box again and brings out a hood, a balaclava, a pair of scissors and some gaffer tape.*

Whit team dae ye support?

BILLY. You know.

KEVIN. For the camera. Celtic or Rangers?

BILLY. Rangers.

KEVIN. Tories or Labour?

BILLY. Neither.

KEVIN. Dae ye believe in God?

BILLY. Dae I fuck.

KEVIN. Catholics or Protestants?

BILLY. Protestants.

KEVIN. Where've ye been for the last two year?

BILLY. Iraq.

KEVIN. And why d'ye come home?

BILLY. I'm on leave.

KEVIN. So when're ye due back?

BILLY. Next week.

KEVIN. Why d'ye join the Army, Billy?

BILLY. I wis bored.

KEVIN. Whit else?

BILLY. That's it. (*Beat*.) I wanted tae get away fae here, away
fae this. Ma life is fucking boring, man. I'm nothing here.
Jist wan big fuck-all.

See, when I wis in Iraq, Kev, they used tae call us Billy the
Hun, ye know? Cos I wis always going on aboot the Rangers
and that. And I says tae them wan time, hey, it's Mister
Orange tae you, okay? And so they started calling us Mister
Orange. It wis alright, ye know? I didnae mind it. But then
they all had tae have a name as well. Danny Medallion,
Peggy Sue, Doctor Des, Smoky Bacon, Scotty the Dog
Lover, DJ Jim the Disco King. Bunch of fucking jokers.

I'm no going back there. I don't care whit they dae tae me.
I'm no going back.

Sometimes we took wan of the guys for a walk, ye know?
Wan of the Iraqis. We took them tae wan of the trucks. We
called it the disco truck. That wis a laugh. Cos big Jim, he'd

set it up wae speakers and that. Big fuck-off speakers in the
back of this truck. Like a big metal container. And we'd stick
the guy in there for a few hours. Just lock the door and take
turns picking the tunes. I used tae like sticking on some
happy hardcore. Or a wee bit of thrash metal. But see, Dave,
dickhead Dave, he wis a cunt. He used tae put on *Bob the
Builder*, the *Teletubbies* and that. All this kiddies' shite, ye
know? If we got bored, we'd jist put the song on a loop and
go away for a couple of hours.

I came doon wan time and big Jim had left a guy in there all
night listening tae 'Why dae birds suddenly appear' by The
Carpenters. When I opened the door, there's this fucking guy
lying there. I wis like that tae big Jim, here, that's cruel.
Imagine making somebody listen tae that pish. That's
fucking sick.

D'ye want tae know something funny? I've got photographs.

KEVIN. Whit kind of photographs?

BILLY. Photographs that naebody's allowed tae see. Private
photographs. That's ma project, eh? Everybody's got some
kind of project. Well that's mine.

KEVIN *ties* BILLY *to a chair using the gaffer tape.*

KEVIN. I went doon tae the bookies this morning.

BILLY. D'you hear whit I jist says?

KEVIN. Did you no hear me? I says, I went doon the bookies.

BILLY. Did ye?

KEVIN. Aye.

BILLY. I thought it wis yer day aff.

KEVIN. That's right.

BILLY. So why d'ye go doon there?

KEVIN. I went doon tae lay a bet.

BILLY. Win anything?

KEVIN. Nut.

KEVIN *pulls a golf club out of the box.*

I took this wae me.

BILLY. I didnae know you played golf.

KEVIN. I don't.

BILLY. Whit's that for then?

KEVIN. I smashed the place up. The windaes, the tellies, the computers, the tills, the display boards, the one-armed bandits, everything. The illusion. It's all fucked. They had tae close it doon. I stopped them stealing the auld guys' money, eh? I put them oot of business.

BILLY. That wis pretty stupid.

KEVIN. Naw it wisnae.

BILLY. They'll jist open it up again.

KEVIN. And I'll close them doon again.

BILLY. You'll get the sack.

KEVIN. I quit.

BILLY. You'll get the jail.

KEVIN. Naw, that's the best bit. D'ye want tae know the best bit? That's the funniest thing aboot it. They didnae know it wis me.

He puts on the balaclava.

Cos I wis wearing a disguise.

KEVIN *laughs.* BILLY *slowly starts to laugh too. They both laugh.* BILLY *stops laughing.* KEVIN *breaks down in tears from the laughter.*

BILLY. That wis good.

KEVIN. D'ye like that wan?

BILLY. Aye, that wis very good.

KEVIN. Did ye like it?

BILLY. Aye.

KEVIN. Did ye?

BILLY. That wis very funny. (*Beat*.) That's whit I like aboot
you, Kev, I can always rely on you for a good laugh.

KEVIN *stops laughing.*

KEVIN. That's right, eh? Kevin the joker. Kevin the clown.
Naebody ever takes me seriously. No ma sister. No ma
friends. No even you.

KEVIN *puts the hood over* BILLY*'s head. He struggles to
throw it off but is strapped tight to the chair.* KEVIN *puts on
a cassette tape of angry adolescent rock and dances to the
music. He takes out the gun and postures for the video
camera. After a while he takes the hood off* BILLY*'s head
and points the gun in his face.*

BILLY. That wisnae funny, Kev. I could've fucking suffocated.

KEVIN. How could ye have? Ye can put these on a prisoner for
seventy-two hours before it starts tae become inhumane.

BILLY. I'm no a fucking prisoner.

KEVIN. Naw, you're an illegal combatant.

BILLY. Whit d'ye want, Kev?

KEVIN. You know whit I want. It's simple. I want the truth.

BILLY. I've told ye everything. That's all there is.

KEVIN. Whit did ye tell me? Some pish aboot Iraq. I don't gie
a fuck aboot that. The whole world's at war, mate, in case ye
hidnae noticed. Islam against the West. We woke up wan
morning and – boom, boom – the great jihad wis begun. And
the front line, Billy, isnae in Iraq, or Iran, or Syria, or
Afghanistan. It's here. It's where we live. The real enemy is
the enemy within.

BILLY. You're fucking tripping.

KEVIN. This is a war zone, get it? And in a war zone people
get hurt. People like me. People like you. And people like ma
sister.

BILLY. Where is she? Whit have ye done tae her?

KEVIN. Whit have you done tae her? That's whit I want tae know.

KEVIN *presses the gun into* BILLY*'s head.*

BILLY. Don't be stupit, Kev.

KEVIN. No hard feelings, man. I jist want tae gie ye a gift, that's all. I want tae give the gift of martyrdom.

BILLY. Stop it. It's no funny. Turn aff the video.

KEVIN. D'ye no want tae be a martyr for the cause?

BILLY. I don't even know whit the fucking cause is.

KEVIN. Ah! Ladies and gentlemen of the jury, I rest my case. I hereby declare the defendant guilty.

BILLY *shakes frenetically in his chair.*

Ye know something, Billy, I'm gonnae enjoy killing you. I don't even need a reason. I'm jist gonnae dae it for the sheer fuck ae it.

BILLY. Help!

KEVIN. Who d'ye think's listening? Them next door? They don't gie a fuck. Naebody's gonnae come running. It jist sounds like I'm watching a film on the telly.

BILLY. Help!

KEVIN. And they'll no hear the gun fire, Billy, cos I'm no gonnae shoot ye. Naw, that's too easy.

He puts down the gun and picks up the Polaroid camera.

Whit I want tae dae is far more biblical. (*Beat.*) I'm gonnae cut yer fucking heid aff.

BILLY. Help!

KEVIN. Smile for the camera.

KEVIN *takes a picture.* BILLY *starts convulsing.* KEVIN *backs away in disgust.* BILLY *slips into unconsciousness.*

KEVIN *lays the photograph down to develop. He picks up the pair of scissors and cuts the tape around* BILLY*'s wrists and ankles. Then he lowers his 'body' onto the floor. He turns off the video camera and tidies up the mess created by their 'execution' game.*

You hungry, Billy? I'm starving. D'ye want a fried egg? The bread's a bit stale. But I might have a tin of beans. Wait here and I'll go and have a look.

He goes towards the kitchen.

And don't you go anywhere. I'll be right back.

Exit KEVIN. BILLY *stirs, a little at first, then he wakes. Slowly, he stands up. He hears* KEVIN *in the kitchen and heads for the door. It's locked. He spots the gun and picks it up.*

Here, Billy, listen tae this. (*Reading.*) Mercury's conjunction wae Neptune proves that your assumptions can turn oot tae be wrong. Often the greatest surprises arise from the most familiar situation. All ye need tae dae is keep yer eyes and ears open.

KEVIN *comes back into the room, reading a tabloid newspaper.*

There's got tae be something in this, eh?

He looks up and sees BILLY *with the gun.*

BILLY. Come here.

BILLY *gestures for* KEVIN *to sit in the chair.*

KEVIN. D'ye want tae hear yours? Whit star sign are you again? Oh aye, that's right. Taurus. (*Reading.*) Jupiter, the planet of hope, is changing direction in the sky, allowing you tae change direction in yer life. Suddenly, you are becoming aware of keys ye could turn. Doors ye could open. And possibilities ye could explore.

BILLY *presses the gun to* KEVIN*'s head.*

Well?

BILLY. Well?

KEVIN. Go on, dae something, Billy. It's your line.

BILLY. Give us the keys.

KEVIN. I don't know where they are. I must've left them in the kitchen.

BILLY. Give us the fucking keys.

KEVIN. Whit ye gonnae dae, shoot me?

BILLY. Now!

KEVIN *takes the keys out of his pocket and lifts his hands above his head.*

KEVIN. Swap ye.

BILLY. Naw. Put them on the telly. Then walk away. Slowly.

KEVIN *goes to the television and places the keys on top.*

Now fucking move.

KEVIN. Well, well, well, the tables have turned, eh? Ye'd never guess you were a soldier, Billy. That gun disnae suit ye. Nae wunner they threw ye out.

BILLY. Shut up.

BILLY *picks up the keys, still aiming the gun at* KEVIN, *and goes to the door.*

KEVIN. I left the egg cooking on the stove. I better go and check them, eh?

BILLY. Don't you fucking go anywhere.

BILLY *unlocks the door. He throws the keys on the floor.*

Pick them up.

KEVIN *bends down.*

Wae yer teeth.

He drops to his knees and lowers his mouth towards the keys.
BILLY *kicks his backside.* KEVIN *falls flat on the floor.*

KEVIN. Feel better noo?

BILLY. Naw.

KEVIN. That no enough for ye? D'ye want more?

BILLY. Aye, there's something else I want.

KEVIN. Whit?

BILLY. Turn on the camera. And give it tae me.

Reluctantly, KEVIN *switches the video camera to record and hands it to* BILLY.

Sit doon. (*Beat.*) Speak.

KEVIN. Whit d'ye want me tae say?

BILLY. I want you tae tell me whit ye did tae yer sister.

KEVIN. I didnae dae a thing tae ma sister. You're the wan…

BILLY. Whit the fuck did ye dae tae her?

KEVIN. I told ye. She's in the kitchen.

BILLY. Naw she's no.

KEVIN. Go and look for yersel. Or are ye too scared?

BILLY. Shut up.

KEVIN. On ye go. Ya fucking pussy.

BILLY. Shut it or I'll shoot you in the face.

KEVIN. Go ahead, Billy. We're all gonnae die anyway.

BILLY. I'm no gonnae die.

KEVIN. Course ye are. Me, you, the whole fucking species. Our time has come. Everybody says so. Scientists. Prophets. It says so in the Bible. The judgement day is coming, quick.

BILLY. Where dae you get all this shite?

KEVIN. I'm telling ye. I saw it on the telly. We're gonnae bomb each other aff the face of the planet.

BILLY. I don't gie a fuck aboot that. Jist tell me where yer sister is. Where's Pamela?

KEVIN. Pamela's gone.

Pause.

BILLY. Ye know whit I think? I think you don't even know where she is, dae ye? You huvnae got a fucking clue.

KEVIN. None of that matters, Billy. Have you no been listening? I want tae die. Go ahead and shoot me. Dae it for Pamela. That's it. I'm ready.

Long pause. BILLY *throws down the gun.*

BILLY. There's no bullets, ya fucking diddy.

He goes to the door.

KEVIN. Where are you going?

BILLY. I'm gonnae look for your sister.

He exits.

KEVIN. You'll be back. Ye hear me, Billy? You'll be back. I know ye will.

Pause.

You'll be back.

KEVIN *puts on the video of* PAMELA *and stares at the screen. The sound of fire travels through from the kitchen.*

Lights fade.

The End.

THE PRICE OF A FISH SUPPER

Catherine Czerkawska

Catherine Czerkawska is a widely published writer of novels, short stories, poems and award-winning plays for the stage and for BBC Radio 4 (some two hundred hours of radio drama to date). She has just come to the end of a Royal Literary Fund Writing Fellowship at the University of the West of Scotland. Her stage play about Chernobyl, *Wormwood*, was produced to critical acclaim at the Traverse Theatre and is now a set text for Scottish Higher Drama. *The Secret Commonwealth*, her third play for Òran Mór, in Glasgow, was produced in February 2010. *The Price of a Fish Supper* was written for the same venue and subsequently staged at the Edinburgh Festival Fringe and broadcast on BBC Radio 4. It was followed by *Burns on the Solway*, a play about the final days of the poet's life.

Her third novel *The Curiosity Cabinet* (Polygon, 2005) was one of three finalists for the Dundee Book Prize, and her non-fiction book, *God's Islanders*, a major hardback study of the history and landscape of the Isle of Gigha, was published by Birlinn in November 2006. She has just completed a new novel called *The Summer Visitor*, and – among much else – is revising *The Sorrel Mare* and working on a novel, titled *The Physic Garden*.

Catherine lives in rural Ayrshire with her artist husband Alan Lees.

The Price of a Fish Supper was first performed at Òran Mór, Glasgow, as part of the A Play, a Pie and a Pint season on 28 March 2005, with the following cast:

RAB	Paul Morrow
Director	Gerda Stevenson

Characters

RAB

Author's Note

The set consists of the detritus of the fishing industry: wooden and plastic boxes, odds and ends of rope, nets, old tyres. But not too much of any of it. Or maybe none of it. This could be played anywhere, in a pub or a club and with no set at all.

Rab is a middle-aged man. He may look older than he is. He's slightly the worse for wear.

He has to take us with him on a journey which may or may not be one of redemption.

Pauses are as long or as short as Rab likes to make them. They only indicate breaks in his thought processes.

Also the punctuation is important. Where there are no full stops it is because the idea runs on.

And line endings matter too. On the other hand, it's all open to interpretation.

RAB

Are you after a fry?
You'll be lucky.

Folk used to say that.
Have you got a fry?
Dog's abuse.
Now you'd get dog's abuse.

There are lucky fishermen
And there are unlucky fishermen.
My grandfather was lucky.
My great-grandfather was lucky.
King Herring.

When Willie's sittin in the stern, wi the wire, feelin for the
herrin
Shouts to Kruger keep her west, I've felt all night but this is the
best...

Pause.

They used to
they used to come down the harbour. After a fry. People like you.
Holiday folk. When the harbour was busy.

My grandfather Fergie
His name was Fergie but they aye called him Jeely Piece.
He used to tell me
he'd a cousin who was harbour master down here and he used
to feed the gulls every morning with guts from the herring
and this wee Glasgow woman comes down all dolled up
she looks at the seagulls and says are those your pigeons?
Of course they are, Madam, he says. I'm just feeding them.
Could I buy two of them, she asks him.
Oh, certainly he replies.
She hands him five bob and he pockets it and says just take your
pick, missus.

Pause.

Have you got the price of a fish supper?
Have you?
No.
So what do you think I'm going to spend it on?
Aye, well, you might be right.
But let's face it I am no longer a young man so does it matter?
Does it matter?

It is an ancient mariner and he stoppeth one of three.
For all averred I had killed the bird that made the breeze to
blow.
Used to say that at the school.
Do you know what a fucking albatross looks like?
They're big.
That's what they are.
Fucking gigantic.

Funny word that.
Albatross.
The more you say it the funnier it gets.
Albatross.
They don't write them like that any more.
Instead of the cross the albatross about my neck was hung.
Used to have to learn it off by heart.
They don't nowadays.
Not by heart.

This year next year some time
time goes by
too fucking fast for me.

You count in tens don't you? You say in ten years' time I'll be
And then you think, one time you think how many?
How many ten years do I have left?
Three lots, two lots, one lot?
Water water everywhere and not a drop

Nicky Jock, he fell off the quayside, dead drunk, went crashing
down between the boat and the wall.
They found him in the morning floating face down.
That was a few years ago now.

He was only thirty.
He didn't have many tens did he?
Not that I'm planning my exit you understand. Not right now,
anyway.

But I'll tell you what.
I have to try something else something new.
In ten years' time I'll be
I'll not be sitting here anyway.
One way or another
I have to take myself
I have to give myself a
except that when I try it all goes
the sea's in my head.
It's quiet down here. Nice and peaceful. At least there's that.

I could work on a ferry. Or take folk out fishing. Rod fishing.
The sea's in everything I
The sea.
The great fucking weight of it holding you down.

Pause.

Fish. They were always going on about the price of fish.
In the shops. In the market. The price of a fish supper.
Gies a fry, son.
Once upon a time you could give them a few fish.
But later on we were supposed to say no, not a hope in hell.
Why, they'd say. Why can't we buy it?
But see it all goes away and then it gets processed and
packaged so the last thing it looks like is a fish.
And then it comes back and then you can buy it,
in the shops like.
Frozen or chilled. Fish fucking fingers.

We weren't supposed to sell it but
sometimes I did.
And sometimes I'd give them a fry for nothing.
If I liked the look of them. If they were polite.
If they didn't piss me off. If they were female.

Jimmy. He said I was giving the profits away.

Fuck's sake, half of it goes to Spain.
They eat fish you wouldn't look at. In Spain.
They eat stuff that looks more like it should be in a pet shop in Spain.
They barbecue them and suck the brains out of the prawns in Spain.
They eat velvet swimmer crabs in Spain and they're so small you wouldn't think

But who are we to complain?
Do we complain?
Aye. We do. All the time. Who doesn't?
But if they pay for the shit it's fine by me
he used to say.
That's what Jimmy used to say. Jimmy.
Jimmy's my
Was my
Was

Pause.

Would you just take a look at this place?
You'd never think this was once a working harbour would you?
A hundred boats and more.
You could walk across it on the decks of boats.
Mind you that was before my time.
Now there's... well... see for yourself.
They moved the market.
The water's full of turds and plastic bags.
Going through the motions eh?
You wouldn't believe the plastic bags and the shopping trolleys.
Why do folk have this urge to dump shopping trolleys in the river?
Or do they just
like lemmings
after dark?

Pause.

My great-grandfather was King Herring.
Best fisherman of his day.
But that was when there were fish to be had.

There's this story my grandfather used to tell me.
There they are, steaming up Loch Striven. It's a lovely evening.
And the whole land just seems to disappear.
They steam into this haze and you know what it is?
It's herrings.
Putting up.
That's what they call it.
Breathing.
And it covers the whole sea like a mist.
The sea's covered in it.
The herring have just arrived and they've been
swimming hard and fast... and they're
putting up and you can just see it.

Or you would see gannets
streckin' on the herring below
diving into the water.

They go blind. Gannets. Did you know that?
They go blind and when they can't do the business any more
they die.
They die of starvation.

I've seen the fire on the water.
I've seen that.
Phosphorescence.
Light everywhere.
You pee over the side and it's like
Magic.
But no more.
I haven't seen it for years.
They say it was. It was
that was the way it was.
But it's gone. It's all gone now.

The herring went and they never came back.

Pause.

Some say it's the overfishing and some say it's the pollution and
some say it's the nets and – what the fuck?
Some say.
I say hell mend them all.

They sold this industry down the river.
And I'll tell you another thing
we went a damn sight more quietly than the miners
too busy trying to earn a living.
But that's not
no.
That's another story.
That isn't why I'm

Pause.

What I wanted to tell you was this.
What I really wanted to tell you was
it's in a fucking museum you know.
It looks.
Well you wouldn't want to.
You wouldn't ever want to
what I'm trying to tell you
the last time I was there, Christ, the only time I was
ever there, there were kids.
A bunch of kids.
All over it.
They were on a day out from somewhere.
School kids.
You couldn't blame them. No. Oh no.
They were having this brilliant day out.
One of them says
I hear him.
This is brilliant he says
Cool.
Cool they say.
You wouldn't even want to
I don't know what the fuck to do about it.
I don't know what to do or what to say.
I haven't the words.
Who the fuck would ever have the words?

Pause.

Jesus Christ alone knows why I went.
I paid my ticket as well.
I paid.

I can't remember what it cost.
What it cost
It cost
The price of a fish supper.

I didn't tell them.
I mean if I'd told them they'd have gone all soft.
I wouldn't have had to pay.
I know that.
Well I'm assuming that but who knows?
Who knows eh?
They might have made me pay.

Anyway I did pay.
They've got
they've got a notice.
Telling you.
Telling you all about

Who wrote it I wonder?
How would they write it?
No I mean how could they?
Did they think?
Did they know?

So I get there and it's full of kids having an experience.
It looks like. I can't tell you. It looks like some
great big like a sickness.
Sitting there.
Just sitting there. High and dry.

Come to that it doesn't look dry.
Not at all fucking dry.
Even on a sunny day it looks kind of wet.
Oozing.
Like a big sore.
In me.
A sore sore place.
It hurts
me.

Pause.

I'm not making much sense am I?
I will tell you. I will. If you'll wait with me.
Wait a minute.

If it was farmers
Jesus, don't get me started about
If it was farmers or miners at least they'd
But they didn't did they?
We're all in the same boat really.
Nobody.
Nobody gives a fuck and that's the truth.
Jimmy says. No. Jimmy said.
I keep saying that you see.
Jimmy says. Jimmy does. Jimmy thinks.
Jimmy might.
Jimmy wouldn't. Jimmy doesn't. Jimmy won't.
Not ever. Never again.
Jimmy and Annie. Annie and Jim. Jimmy and me.
My brother. Myself.

Pause.

We were at the school together. Me, Jimmy, Annie.
Annie was my friend. My pal. Mine.

The school. Picture it.
It's just a wee school.
But there's this long corridor. With classrooms off it.
It smells of chalk. Cabbage. Sweaty shoes. Disinfectant. Piss.
The first day I go in the front door and I can smell all this.
And I'm off running and I'm straight out the back.
Away home.
Mammy mammy, I'm home.
That's it. I've done school. Over. Finished.

One day. All done.
I don't know why I don't twig. Jim's older. He goes every day.
I know he goes. I see him go. I wave him off.
But no me I think. No me.
What am I like?

My mother's mortified.
But she keeps me at home that day.

She's in the middle of the weekly wash.
Place full of steam and sunlight soap.
She sits me down with a glass of Irn Bru.
Be good, Robbie, she says.
Be a good boy for your mammy now.

My dad's raging when he comes home from the boat but my
mammy won't let him batter me.

The second day they lock the door at the back so I can't get out.
They put me in a classroom and I sit at this wooden desk with
initials and rude words cut into it.
Except that I can't read them because I can't read, can I?
I only find out they're rude later on like.
I'm greetin I'm making a bloody awful racket.
They take me out to the cloakroom with its wee
pegs for coats and they give me a
glass of water but I just keep on greetin.
They sit me in a chair and I fall asleep.
I just shut it all out and fall asleep until home time.

The third day I have the wood axe, the
short-handled one for chopping up the
kindling under my grey wool V-neck jumper.
I'm all for breaking out the back door.

Jimmy, he's in Primary Three.
He's mortified as well.
He says he'll hammer me if I do it again.
He says I'll beat the living daylights out of you.

The next day they sit me beside Annie.
It's their last shot.
Their best shot.
She's wee and plump with plaits and nice pink cheeks.
She watches me howling for a bit and she says
For goodness' sake!
like a grown woman.
She's five and already she's got this I don't know this
self-possession.
She sorts me out.
She tells me what to do and when to do it and how to do it.

Nobody ever picks on me.
Annie's got a temper.
I feel safe with Annie.
Annie always sorts me out.
Well she used to. She did. She did.

Pause.

I spend Saturdays with my granddad.
It's my reward for putting up with the school.
He builds me this wooden fishing boat in the
garden out of old fish boxes just.
He tells me all about the herring drifters that
bought the herring from the fishing fleet.
But the way he tells it I know it's all by, finished, over.
He knows all their names.
*Karina. Karrier. Watchful. Challenger. Good Design. Gael
Maree.*
I'm talking about years ago. Before the wars.
My great-grandfather's time.
King Herring.
They called it the years of the big fishings.
It was never like that when I was.
Never.
Only I think the stories my granddad told me made me
I wanted it to be I wanted that
life. I wanted
the way it was.

He's long gone.
He died while I was just a wee lad.
My dad chopped the boat up for kindling.
The boat he made me.
Grow up, Robbie, he said, grow up.

Pause.

We go to the big school.
Annie's in 1A, 2A, 3A.
I'm in 1D, 2D, 3D.

Annie's brilliant. Everyone says Annie's brilliant.
She's going in for teacher training.

She's not plump any more. Something's happened.
She's tall and slim with long legs and shiny hair.

I'm going in for being a gorilla. A numpty.
What they call neds now.
Non-educated delinquents.
I'm going in for the all-time record for being belted.
I'm well on the way to getting it.
The skin on the palms of my hands is like leather
so I never flinch.
I don't give a stuff.
Wee Mary teaches maths. She belts me every day.

I watch the way her
nostrils flare when she brings the strap down on my
crossed hands.
She's enjoying it.
So I smile at her.
Thanks, Miss. I say. Thanks, Miss.
One day I reckon I'll take that belt and smack her across her
fucking weasel face with it.
But I don't. I do nothing. I just take it.
We all take it.

Last year I saw her in town. In a café.
Drinking tea and eating a baked potato.
She was this little old woman dressed in grey, all shrivelled up
and she didn't recognise me why would she
and I couldn't bring myself to speak to her.
I couldn't say a word to her.
I just ignored her.
Walked away.
You'd think it wouldn't matter at this distance in
You'd think I might have forgotten but

Anyway, my dad comes ashore.
A steel warp clatters him across the hand
He nearly loses his fingers.
He can't be doing with the cold and the long hours any more.
He sells carpets.
He smokes like a lum.

Annie's fifteen and I'm still fourteen.
There's about five months between us.
There's all of 3B and 3C between us.
I'm a wee squirt still.
My voice hasn't even broken.
Jimmy's eighteen and he's at the fishing with
money burning a hole in his pocket.

We're in this cafe.
The Café Sorrento. On the main street.
Everyone goes there. It's the place to be.
We're eating ice creams. Banana longboats.
And drinking Coke.
Annie's there too.
Jimmy comes in and he starts chatting her up
and I think he hasn't got a
hope in hell because Annie's my pal she always has been but
fuck me she likes it.
He buys her a coffee. Not a Coke but a coffee.
Espresso from a machine.
All foam.
The height of sophistication.
She likes it.
She drinks it.
She likes him.
She talks to me but it's always about him.
He talks to me but it's always about her.
He takes her out. He takes her to the dancing. And there's not a
fucking thing I can do about it.
I borrow cash from my dad who's had a good month with the
carpets and I buy a Beatles jacket and Cuban-heeled boots.
Jimmy laughs at me.
Annie says nice boots but that's all she says.
He doesn't know.
Or he does know and he doesn't care.
I don't fucking know any more.
I hate it.
I don't hate him.
He's my brother.
But I hate it. This.
Him and Annie.

I can't say anything.
I zip my lip and then
I leave school.

Pause.

But we're in the same boat. We're on the same boat.

The *Silver Harvest*. That's my first boat.
Golden Harvest, Golden Dawn, Golden Sheaf,
Christmas Morn, Christmas Rose, Rose Marie,
Mary Jane, Mary Anne, Star of the Sea.
In those days they were the names were
the names were
bonnie names for bonnie boats.
Wood. The tarry smell of wood.

It's Sandy Galbreath has the *Silver Harvest* and they call him
Silver Sanny.
And Jesus he's a hard man.
I'm fifteen, no I'm fourteen if I'm honest
because I bunk off school to do it.
I go aboard her as cook.
Jimmy's a deckhand already. He gets me the place.
Rab'll come aboard he says.
My brother.
My mother's scandalised but my father says why not. It's what
the lad wants to do.
Why should he stay on at the school for six months for no
reason?
Wee Mary's glad to see the back of me.
They're all glad to see the back of me.
Right wee nyaff they think.
Annie says Take care, Rab.
Everything she says
I say it to myself so I remember it.
Daft or what?

So I'm cook. Which is the way you start.
Only I can't cook, can I?
I burn the porridge for two weeks till my mammy takes me in
hand and learns me how to do it.

Bacon rolls. I can do bacon rolls. After a fashion.
Get the tea on, Rab. He yells it from his bunk. Silver Sanny.
Get the fucking tea on. He's a terror in the mornings.
Not just in the mornings either.
Off the boat he's as nice a man as you could wish to meet.
Polite. Pleasant. What a nice man, my mammy says whenever
we meet him ashore.
Don't you believe it says my dad who knows him well.
Only on board he's. Jesus. He turns into a monster.

So what happens is
this day Sandy tells me to get mending, there's a big tear in the
nets, it's fucking enormous we snagged Christ knows what
down there and there's nothing to be done till it's fixed and
I can't mend.
I don't know one end of a netting needle from the other.
And I'm thinking what the fuck can I do? What can I say?
See if you make a stilter you have to cut the piece out and start
all over again and I'll not be popular with the crew if I try it.
So I'm thinking what can I say and

I say no, I'm not doing it and I can see Jimmy on deck going
Christ Almighty what is he about, and Silver Sanny says why
no? And I say just for no. Cos I'm no
and Sandy says get that fucking needle in your hand and mend
the fucking hole you wee… and I'm not for saying I don't know
how, so eventually I say Cooks disnae mend, Sanny. Cooks
disnae mend.

Pause.

It goes dead dead quiet.
I'm expecting him to beat the living daylights out of me
because he's got that reputation like.
But what does he do, he starts laughing.
I think he's going to bust a gut he laughs that much.
Cooks disnae mend, he keeps saying. Cooks disnae mend. Fuck
me cooks disnae fucking mend.
He gets on the radio.
It goes round the whole fleet. Everyone's saying it.
Cooks disnae mend.

Sanny's dead. Stroke carried him off years ago.
One temper tantrum too many.
Stroke in the wheelhouse they said.
Put that kettle on, Rab.
Where's the fucking tea, Rab?
Cooks disnae mend.

So Annie and Jimmy go to the dancing and he takes her out in
his car because he's bought this car by now.
Wee Morris Traveller. Green. With wood. He polishes the wood.
She's into Jim Reeves
on the Dansette.
She likes Jim Reeves and Roy Orbison and Gene Pitney.
They go to the pub and they go to the dancing.
He takes her off in his car and Christ knows what they do in his
car.
Well I know. Me and Christ both. And I don't know about him
but I think about it all the time.

She's friendly with me like. But not. Not like. No.
Aye well. What can I do?
What can I say?
I don't think he even.
I don't think he gives a
Maybe he doesn't know how I feel. Did I ever tell him?
I don't think I ever
No.

Next thing she's got a fucking bun in the oven and she leaves
school and they get married.
My mammy's scandalised.
My dad just laughs.
Her parents are furious but Jimmy's earning good money and
they get married. Don't get me wrong. He wants to get married.

So there's a wedding. And I'm fucking best man.
In a suit. My first proper suit. I look like a kid in fancy dress.
I look at those photos now and there's me in that cheap grey
suit, and there's Annie in one of those straight mini-dresses and
a hat, she looks like Twiggy. She's got this wee bump out in
front where this big pink flower on her dress stretches over her
belly but you can't see it too well in the pictures and there's

Jimmy in a more expensive suit and Annie's wee sister Rose
who looks like Annie only smaller and fatter in a cotton dress
and white ankle socks.

Annie's wee sister knows.
I don't know how she knows but she does.
Not about the baby.
The world and his wife knows about the baby.
Jimmy's that pleased about the baby that he's told everyone.

No. Rose knows about me. The way I feel about Annie.
She's only about eight or nine but she says
Don't you bother about our Annie she's not worth it what's for
you won't go by you and there's plenty more fish in the sea.
I just tell her to mind her own business
because she's younger than me and she's a kid and
I look at her and it's Annie like she was when we were both but
not Annie
now.
No.
Nothing like Annie
now.

Pause.

I'm not a cook any more.
I've been promoted.
I'm a deckhand.
You have to watch out for
scalder.
S'these wee pink jellyfish trailing in the water.
Burns your fingers.
If you're having a pee over the side and you've got it on your
fingers Jesus,
that'll set your gas at a peep as my granny used say.

I've got muscles.
I've got muscles on my muscles and I can lift anything and I've
got a filthy tongue and
the fact is I drink too much.
But I fit in.
I can mend.
I drink down the harbour and I eat fish and chips and I sleep on
the boat.

It's Jimmy's boat by this time but I've got a share in it. He's
doing well for himself.
He goes home to Annie and the kids. Two kids. Two wee girls.
They call me Uncle Rab.
Nice house. Nice things to put in it.

Dad's dead. The smoking finally got to him. He was fine at sea
but when he came ashore it all

I don't smoke.
I do everything else but.
I'll not die from the fags that's for sure.
I go up to the mission for a shower and a cup of tea.
I drink my pay in the harbour bar, eat fish and chips and then I
go back down and sleep it off on the boat.

The way you do it is you clean your teeth in the morning and it
makes you sick and then you clean them again and you feel
better.
Sometimes there's a
sometimes I take a
a lassie down onto the boat
one of the
the harbour lassies.
Short skirts fat legs shiny tops.
Who am I to grumble?
Sometimes I pay her and sometimes she does it for nothing
because it's a cold night and it's a warm bunk
and a cup of tea afterwards and she knows who I am
and I'm not going to beat her up or anything.
I'm not going to want anything too
I'm not going to do anything she doesn't
You know? It's alright.

Annie says.
You have to settle down, Rab.
Time you found yourself a
time you found yourself.

Rose is away at college.
She's going to be a teacher
and she's engaged.
Annie's pissed off. I can see it.

I know her that well.
Annie's stuck at home with the kids.
Nice house
twin-tub washing machine
wool carpets lovely stuff.
Everything she wants everything new.
She's still pissed off.
Her and Jimmy
he doesn't tell me much
even me. Especially me.
See she's
she's ashamed of what he does.
She likes the cash but she's ashamed of
the smell of fish.
She won't come down to the quay in the car to pick him up.
She won't be seen.
She parks the car at the back of the bank and
she makes him
walk up there for his lift home and
he does it too.
I laugh at him. Fuck's sake, Jimmy, I say.
But he does it anyway.
He's still daft about her.
And time goes on and nothing changes.

Pause.

So what happens next is this.
Funny the way it
See we haul this thing in with the net.
It's round and it's flattish and it's made of green plastic. Big.
Oh quite big. Aye.
Big.
There's a serial number on it. Stencilled on it like.
I mean we see it coming up in the net and Jimmy says oh shit
and I say oh fuck.
And everyone says oh fuck. Even the cook.
So we radio the coastguard and they ask us, no they ask Jimmy
to read the serial number off it which he does,
because you can read it. You can.
You can see it quite clearly.

There's a yacht on the radio and they ask him to stand by just in case and we know full well in case of what.

And they say they'll send an escort from the naval base. To take us in.
And they say meanwhile we're to take it to this bay where the water's deep and let it go and they'll send somebody to deal with it, and we say What just let it go and they say Aye.
So there we are heading in slowly. Pissing ourselves.
And we get there, and drop the thing and it fucking well goes off doesn't it?
There's a... There's like a big. Whoosh. A rush of air. Christ I don't know.
It's happened before you've
I just know it was

A detonation

They said it was more of a detonation like, but it's enough to blow the arse out of the boat and we're bloody deaf and there's bits of the fucking boat floating in the water but we're still afloat and Jimmy's going fuck fuck fuck and we get the boat or what's left of it going again and head for the harbour and the lifeboat comes out anyway
A big inflatable.
And we make it with the boat sinking under us.
No joke I'm telling you.
Brown-trousers job.

Then on the evening news on the telly
it says a fishing boat brought up a World War II bomb in its nets.
Annie says I thought you said it was green plastic
And Jimmy says aye it was
And she says With a serial number? I mean she's not daft is she
And he says aye.
And she says do they think we came up the Clyde on a banana boat I mean do they?

Jimmy's just going daft about his boat and he says he's going to make a song and dance about it make a fuss write to his MP and the *Daily Record* because there was a big naval exercise going on and I'm saying cool it wait and see and then the next thing

we know there's this big offer of compensation from the MOD.
Too big to turn down really.
So we zip our lips and carry on.

And that's when crunch time comes.
Because Jimmy wants to use the cash to buy another boat and
Annie says over her dead body.
They have a monumental row about it.
And for once he puts his foot down and he wins
because it's the one thing
his one big thing. The fishing.

But I want to come ashore.
I say I'm pissed off and I'm taking my share of the money.

I'm running with the money.
I'm throwing in the towel.
I'm swallowing the anchor.
I'm hanging up my seaboots.
I'm

I don't know why I do it. We're talking a few years ago now.
And I'm younger than Jimmy and fit enough and things aren't
that bad.
But I'm tired.
I am so fucking tired.
I'm drinking too much and I'm tired of working all hours and
it's long and hard and cold and too fucking lonely by half
And I can't seem to

I just don't want to do it any more.
Or maybe I think if I'm ashore and Jimmy's at sea and Annie's
Do you get my drift?
Or maybe I can see the way things are headed.
Maybe I'm a smart bastard and I can see.

So I come ashore.
Jimmy's generous but I drink the money.
I piss it against the wall.
I just drink earlier and keep going longer that's all.

Jimmy gets a new boat and goes in with a couple of other guys,
and goes to the clams. They work long hours and they don't

make a fortune but he's happy.
Jimmy's always happy at sea.

On the other hand Annie is truly hacked off.
I think she might leave him but she doesn't.
She's not that hacked off.

I think I might see more of Annie but I don't.

When the money's all gone I sober up and
sell things.
I sell cars for a bit, and then I sell insurance and then
I go back to cars and then caravans
and then cars again and then double glazing and then gas and
then cars.
I don't sell much of any of them.
I'm not cut out for it.
I'm a fucking crap salesman I have to say.
Would you buy a used car off me?
No.
Well then.

Pause.

When I'm not trying to sell stuff
I go and hang round the bars down the harbour for company.
I talk to folk about the fishing.

You know what they call me?
They call me the shore skipper.
They've forgotten that I ever went to sea.
Christ I've all but forgotten it myself.
That's the way it is now.
Nobody knows you.
My granddad would be whirling in his grave.

And then one of them – a bit older than the rest – he says that's
Jimmy Galbreath's brother, Rab, and the other says Christ no, is
he?
And they go aye. Aye. That's him.
His father was at the fishing and his grandfather was at the
fishing before him.
Look at him.

And then one of them says Was that cooks disnae mend
and they start laughing and I'm laughing as well
but it isn't very funny.
I want to smash their daft faces in.

Pause.

All this time the industry's going to fuck.
They move the fish market so they can build new flats.
You can't even see the fucking sea from the harbour nowadays.
I passed this foreign couple one day and they said excuse me
where is the sea and I looked around and I thought fuck me
they're right you can't even see the sea.
The boats follow the market but the fish are few.

You can't kill them when they're wee and expect to have them
when they're big, says my granddad.
But there's more to it than that.
I know there's a lot more to it than that but I just can't
I don't have the words to
It's all here in my head
But I don't have the words
And more time passes.

I sell cars again.
I'm living in a wee council flat in this crap street where half the
houses are boarded up and I sell cars and then they give me the
push because I'm not really selling any cars at all and Jimmy
says for fuck's sake, Rab, come back to sea will you? We're
doing okay. He says it every week for a year. And I tell him to
fuck off. But we don't fall out. No. We don't do that.
He says You're drinking too much, my son, and I tell him to
fuck off again but I know I am.
I'm not about to stop.

I'm not coming to sea with you either, I tell him. You're too
bloody unlucky.

Ah but that's where you're wrong, Rab, he tells me.
Lightning doesn't strike twice. That's what Jimmy says.
We'll be okay now because
lightning doesn't strike twice in the same place
He says.

He thinks.
But it does. It fucking does.
You know.
If they've got it in for you it strikes till you're

Pause.

What happens is this.
This is what I want to tell you.
The whole point is
this is what
this

It's February.
Annie sends Jimmy this big Valentine.
I mean I don't know that at the time do I?
No. But I see it afterwards. I see it.
She says they haven't sent Valentines for years
but this time they do.
He sends her one and she sends him one.
Big soppy things.
Hearts and flowers.
Love and stuff.
Poems in glittery lettering.

The *Annie Rose*. That's the name of the boat.
Annie for Annie and Rose for her wee sister. Jimmy's boat.

You know it now don't you?
You recognise the
don't you remember?
Christ's sake don't you even remember now?

Funny thing is
You hear them. You can hear them.
It's this fucking weird feeling I'm telling you.
You're down below and you can hear this
humming noise. Like machinery. Like an engine.
Like something coming.
Only you go up on deck and there's fuck-all to be seen.
Only sometimes you do see them.
Or just the conning tower.
Tin fish.

They say. Folk say. They say they use the fishing boats. For
positioning or something.
They say shit happens that isn't supposed to happen.
That's for sure.

Whatever
Lightning strikes twice.
They're towing. Jimmy and his crew
aboard the *Annie Rose*.
They snag a sub.
It pulls her down.
Like one minute they're on the surface
And the next
nobody
nobody could do anything.
Too fast.

The *Annie Rose* just goes straight to the bottom.

But even that's not
what I'm trying to say
the night he doesn't come back, when we know there's
something
that's the night Annie… that's the night.
Jesus.
She's. We're.
She only wants Jimmy.
We
only want Jimmy.
Her husband.
My brother.
Oh Jesus Christ my brother.

I keep wondering what happened.
No. I know what happened.
I keep thinking how was it?
That's what I keep asking myself.
Did they know? Did they know what was happening. Christ.
Did they?
Did they have time to think about it. Did they have time to
wonder about anything. Did they have
time to be shit scared before it was
all over?

So what I'm saying is
when they're not back and everyone's going daft looking for the
boat I go to see Annie, and the girls are abroad on holiday and
they haven't got a flight home yet and while he's down there
she starts kissing me and
we go to bed like.
The only time.
The one and only time.
Ever.

Only she doesn't want me does she?
She wants
because I'm like
my brother.
We're not really the same not at all
there's just something.
And I'm sober stone-cold fucking sober
for once but she still doesn't want me.
She wants Jimmy.
So we do it anyway.
And Jimmy's down there.
And in the morning I see two big red hearts, those Valentines
sitting on the mantelpiece.
And afterwards I go and get drunk and I think so that's that.
That's that.
That's that.
Because by then I know
by then we all know.

Oh there's a big fuss. Press. TV. MOD.
I tell reporters from the *Daily Record* the *Daily Mail* the *Sun*
and I forget what else to fuck off and leave us all alone.

They bring them up. Still on board.
I don't think they want to because of the cost but one of the
papers gets a campaign going and there's a picture of Annie and
the girls down the harbour and I reckon they should leave them
where they are but who am I to judge?

They bring them up
and bury them.
The headstone, Christ, the headstone it's this big grey granite
heart with red roses on it you can see it from half a mile away.

It would bust you so it would
like the Valentine.

Mind you it takes a while
So the fishes
the fishes get their own back so to speak.
Well. Some of it.

Pause.

The *Annie Rose.*
It's in a museum now.
What the fuck else could they do with it?
You might have heard of it.
You might even have been to see it.
Lightning does strike twice so don't get too comfortable
will you?

Kids scramble over it and I don't like that.
I don't like folk climbing over it and even into it
down there where they
where Jimmy
saying it's spooky
saying it's cool.
Cool.
It's cool, alright.
It's bloody stone-cold it's a fucking grave.
Now now says the teacher.
A man in cords and a nice shiny leather jacket.

I can hear Jimmy saying leave the kids alone.
They're doing no harm.
But it gives me the
it puts hell into me.

So I go over and say something and they say something back
and then I yell at them and they tell me to fuck off and stop
bothering them and the teacher says now boys.
And it's plain he doesn't know what the hell to do.
Get a life granddad they say. Get a life.
But I'm incensed. I'm incensed.
It all comes out.
I'm totally out of control.

And there's a big stramash.
I don't actually hit anyone. But
I'm yelling and my heart's going like a train.
My head's buzzing.
Lights. I can see wee lights.
I'm drowning.
My cheeks are wet.

The next thing I know they've got the police out to me and they
take me in but then this young cop starts talking to me and he
says I know you, you're cooks disnae mend.
Turns out he's a nephew of Silver Sanny or something.
And when he tells them who I am and who my brother was they
just tell me to go home and behave myself.

He runs me home in the cop car.
He looks mortified. His face is all pink and he goes, I wouldn't
be too happy about it either, pal. I would not.
He leaves me at my own front door and he says
do us a favour, pal.
Just keep away from the place eh?

And I tell him I will. And it's true.
Why else would I go back there?

Pause.

My flat's a pigsty so I come down the harbour.
The mission's closed now been closed for years but there's a
coffee place where the tourists go.
You can sit on a plastic chair with a plastic cup of coffee for
hours.
They don't bother you.
Well they don't bother me.

I think about it all the time. Annie and me. Annie and Jimmy.
Jimmy.
They get you one way or another, don't they?
I have to be sorry for myself because
no one else will be. That's for sure.

Pause.

Rose comes down the harbour.
Annie's sister.
She's surprised to see me.
She's running
Running along the seashore.
She runs in the morning and she runs at night.
I say Why and she just looks puzzled.
It's what I do, she says.
She's a teacher now and what else she's been married and
divorced and no kids like me. She looks younger than she is.
She says I was thinking what a mess they've made of this place.
No boats, no fish market, no nothing.
Flats block the view.
Tourists come down and there's nothing for them to see.
No fish to fry.
Not a fucking thing left.
All that history she says.
She's standing there all sweaty with the running and
She's more furious than I've ever seen her and she reminds me of
Me with the axe
in the school
trying to break out.
Me standing there with the belt coming down on my hands.
Me saying cooks disnae mend
and the herring putting up in the water and
Annie Rose going down down down
and me shouting at a bunch of poor kids who don't know any
better.
Get a life mister. Get a life they said.
We weren't there for the tourists I tell her
and she says no I don't suppose you were.
She sits down next to me.
Let me get my breath back, Robbie, she says.

I tell her
I tell her about the museum.

Bastards she says. Bastards
And for some reason that makes me laugh.

And fuck me she says. When did you last eat anything?
She looks at me and then
she takes hold of my hand.

But I don't do anything because there's nothing left in me.
No way of
it's all gone.
I don't remember things the way I should.
I don't remember.
There's nothing in me. I'm
overfished.
Joke.
I don't have anything left to say.

And after a bit she just runs on.
Bye Robbie she says see you, and I think, aye right.

I'm sitting there with the cold coffee and I remember
there was another boat.
The Summer Rose.
A nice wee canoe-sterned ringer.
A bonnie boat.
Do you mind?
No well you won't but you could never turn against the sun
you were not supposed to turn against the sun.
You would see them down the harbour cantin and cantin
doing it the hard way
so as not to turn against the sun.
Luck was everything.
I mind that.
Only they broke it up.
Nice old boat
But they broke it up and burned it.

Pause.

Oh Wedding Guest this soul hath been
Alone on a wide wide sea
So lonely 'twas that God himself
Scarce seemed there to

Seem-ed. You have to say seem-ed.

See the way I see it I can do one of two things.
I can stay here on the bottom where it's nice and peaceful
with all the weight of the sea to hold me down
Or I can

Where was I? Oh aye.
The Summer Rose.
Turning with the sun.

No
Rose.
Rose just.
What's for you won't go by you she said.

Next thing she comes round to my flat.
I'm gobsmacked.
The door's open I've nothing worth stealing and she comes in.
She falls over a few bottles
and she's frowning and shaking her head
and she says fuck me, Robbie.
I don't believe this.
What a state you're in.

No one calls me Robbie.
Not now.
Her language is almost as bad as mine.
I don't like to hear a woman swear do you?
She's a teacher.
I say do you use the belt and she says no fear. Not allowed now.
Besides
And she stops.
She kind of shrugs like she's saying why
why would I want to?
She's just looking at me.
I say do you swear at the kids like this and she says what do you
think, Robbie?
She tells me how she teaches the what does she call them the
remedial classes and this kid said shit and she said don't say
that word and he said you say it all the time miss and she said
no I don't, I say shite.
Shite.

She's got this parcel in her hand and it smells of warm
newspaper and hot grease and vinegar.
Listen, she says. You have to eat.
I don't care what you do but you have to eat.
She puts the parcel down on the table and she holds me close.

I can smell her and she smells very nice. Clean. I'm not at all clean.

To tell you the truth I need a shave and I need a bath.

I may even have pissed myself.

I smell like shite.

But she kisses me anyway.

Not a kiss like… no. Not like Annie. Not like the harbour lassies. Nothing like any of them.

But a wee peck like your mother gives you. On the cheek. Nice and warm.

My eyes are watering with the vinegar.

Oh Robbie, she says.

Look, she says, I've brought you a fish supper.

The End.

BETTER DAYS BETTER KNIGHTS

A Brief Morality Play

Stanley Eveling

Stanley Eveling was born in Newcastle upon Tyne and wrote his first performed play when he was seven. It contained little dialogue and much rough-and-tumble and was banned by the school authorities. For the next thirty or more years he spent his time in the infantry during the Second World War, and then at Durham and Oxford Universities, studying English Literature and then Philosophy. He went on to teach the latter at Aberdeen and Aberystwyth, and then finally Edinburgh, where he lived for fifty years. He was, for a number of years, the television critic for the *Scotsman,* which followed his delayed return to playwriting. After a spell writing plays for radio he moved to writing for the theatre, where his play *The Balachites* was the first British work to be produced at the newly opened Traverse Theatre. His other plays for the Traverse include *The Buglar Boy and His Swish Friend*, *The Dead of Night*, *Union Jack (and Bonzo)*, *Caravaggio*, *Buddy*, *Our Sunday Times*, *Dear Janet Rosenberg, Dear Mr Kooning*, *The Lunatic, the Secret Sportsman and the Woman Next Door* and *Come and Be Killed*. His most recent play, *Ways to Remember*, received a rehearsed reading at the Traverse in June 2009. He also wrote poetry and was engaged on a philosophical work called *On Practically Everything*. He was married with four children and ten grandchildren. He died on 24 December 2008.

Better Days Better Knights was first performed at the Pool
Lunch-Hour Theatre, Hanover Street, Edinburgh, in November
1971, with the following cast:

KNIGHT   Tony Haygarth
WATER SPRITE   Sue Carpenter

It was revived at the King's Head Theatre, London, in 1976 in a
production directed by Max Stafford-Clark.

Characters

KNIGHT

WATER SPRITE

The scene is a pleasant one. The KNIGHT *sitting on a rocky outcrop, the* WATER SPRITE *on a grassy knoll. He is in shining armour, she in whatever Sprites wear when not immersed, something pretty fetching anyway. She trails her fingers in flowing water! A long pause to give the audience time to take in this incredible scene. Then the* KNIGHT *lifts off his helmet, scratches his balding head, wipes his brow, puts his helmet on again or doesn't, sighs and tries to make himself comfortable, then:*

KNIGHT. I don't quite foller yer argument.

The SPRITE *sighs. Begins to comb her flowing tresses.*

I mean, suppose we did get married...

SPRITE. Yes...

She speaks in a somewhat detached, matter-of-fact way as Sprites will. After all, she is not human.

KNIGHT. What would be the advantage of it?

She stares at him with big Water-Sprite eyes.

As I see it... we could have a very nice working relationship as it is...

The SPRITE *continues to give him the staring treatment.*

Beside the fact I'm very rarely in one place for any length of time, I mean, the sort of work I do, the nature of it...

SPRITE (*explains*). It would mean I would become an human being, you see.

She speaks very correctly, I think. As one who has made painful efforts to speak human.

KNIGHT. A cry for help here, succour there... Dragons!

SPRITE. I would acquire the capacity to suffer...

KNIGHT. Married to me, you mean?

SPRITE. Exactly.

Pause.

KNIGHT. What was it you said you were?

SPRITE. When?

KNIGHT. Before... you know... when we was discussing...

SPRITE. I am a Water Sprite.

KNIGHT. Ah... ah... Er... what does that entail... exactly?

SPRITE. Dunno.

KNIGHT. Mm. A Water Sprite, eh? Huh! Nobody tells me anything. Can you swim underwater?

SPRITE. I think so.

KNIGHT. Without breathing, I mean?

SPRITE. Do human beings breathe underwater?

KNIGHT. No, I meant –

SPRITE. I'm not sure. I can't remember. I must be able to, I suppose. I would not be much of a Water Sprite if I couldn't breathe underwater, would I?

KNIGHT. You see, when I first met your parents... well, your foster parents, that is, no mention was made of you being a Water Sprite. They said you were wild, of course, and much given to running on the printless marges, leastways that's how your father put it, but neither of them bothered to mention the fact that you were a Water Sprite. Which is somewhat remiss of them, not to put too fine a point on it.

SPRITE. I'm sorry.

KNIGHT. Puts me in a bit of a predicament, you see. Knightly code and that. Courtesy, honour. Puts me in a bit of a cleft stick.

SPRITE. You do not have to if you do not want to.

KNIGHT. Ah, well, that's the point, as I see it. I mean, I do want to. I'm keen on it even... but... I have prior commitments, you see...

SPRITE. I just thought I would ask.

KNIGHT....though, mind you, speaking strictly *entre nous*, I have the sneaking suspicion that the days of the knight are numbered, if you see what I mean.

He laughs.

SPRITE. No.

KNIGHT. Mm... I don't suppose Water Sprites laugh very much, do they?

SPRITE. We do not laugh at all.

KNIGHT. Really? I like a good laugh meself.

SPRITE. Nor weep.

KNIGHT. What you lose on the swings you gain on the roundabouts, as it were.

SPRITE. Yes.

KNIGHT. Never rains but it pours. I've got Bucephalus practically on the sick list... broke pastern he had, festering fetlock... (*Savagely.*) I've a good mind to pack it all in...

The SPRITE *quietly hums to herself.*

(*Savagely.*) Jack the whole lot in. I mean, I mean... regard this armour, it's falling to bits... this plume's seen better days... better knights as well, I imagine... As for under this polish... see... one blow and kaput... one fiery breath, the whole lot'd go up in smoke, disintegrate. Job lot, you see. Second hand. Don't know who it belonged to. Where it's been! Still, mustn't grumble. Huh. I see you like music, then?

SPRITE. I don't know.

KNIGHT. It's just that I noticed you hum quite a lot.

SPRITE. Yes.

KNIGHT. That's why I thought you must like music... because I noticed you frequently hum.

SPRITE. I know.

KNIGHT. Well, then?

SPRITE. What now, Sir Knight?

KNIGHT. Well... well... aaaaagh! (*Totally disgusted.*) I mean it's all very well you suggesting we get married and all that... but... but... what sort of married life do you think we would have? Eh? Me going on about me tourneys and having to rush off at short notice to knock off a few dragons or monsters, even, and you just humming all the time... You can't found an abiding human relationship on that.

She stares at him.

Can you? Can you?

She shakes her head.

You see. And in any case... you being exempt from suffering... though it's hard to credit, you have the eyes for it... I don't really see the harm in us... in... in... mmm... either way, it's immaterial isn't it?

SPRITE. I have to become human.

KNIGHT. Aaaaaah... you don't know what you're saying, being human, it's not all that much... really... I mean, I don't think you'd like it... Here...

SPRITE. What?

KNIGHT. ...it wouldn't work the other way round...?

SPRITE. How do you mean?

KNIGHT. What I've got in mind is, I'm not really keen on water, I'm not really brought up to it. City man, myself, you know, I can manage a sort of breaststroke if I'm pushed but anything elaborate... underwater acrobatics, that kind of thing... I've not got the body for it...

SPRITE. Getting married to me would not make any difference to you.

KNIGHT. Ah.

SPRITE. Only to me. I would change. Instantly.

KNIGHT. Uhu.

SPRITE. They do say human beings came from the sea, originally.

KNIGHT. That a fact.

He practises a few sword thrusts.

SPRITE. They do say human beings are mainly composed of the element out of which they came. Is that true?

KNIGHT. Can't say. Never give it a thought.

SPRITE. What are you doing, Knight?

KNIGHT. Just a few knightly exercises, keep in trim... always at the ready.

SPRITE. You must be very brave, Sir Knight.

KNIGHT. Goes without saying.

SPRITE. Have you made many killings?

KNIGHT. Er... ooh... don't keep a tally, really. Not my style. Some do. Notches on the sword blade, red dots on their pommels... Always thought that was a bit ostentatious, all that.

SPRITE. How do such mortal encounters arise?

KNIGHT. Ah... well, a serious answer to a serious question touching knightly honour, etc.... it's all laid down, you see, it's all technical. If you do anything wrong, anything out of line, you see, it's declared a no contest... That is why I always keep this little book of mine handy.

SPRITE. What does it say?

KNIGHT. This, my dear, is *The Merry Red Book of Courtesy and Good Bearing, with Many Sundrie Goodlie Instructions in the Ways of Jousting and Tourneys...* Bit of a mouthful, really, but it's not too difficult to foller. Take the case of me sitting here on this stone talking to you. We're minding our own business when all of a sudden 'clip, clop,' and looking up I perceive, hoving up on the horizon, a knight, like me but for one significant detail, this one is all in black, see. He has this jet-black hair, his armour is all black and he is called the Black Knight.

Now let us say he is in thrall to a Creature of Evil, so it is his task to seek out good Christom and Right Courteous Knights of Our Lady and belt the daylights out of them, that is, do them to death in mortal encounter, like the book says. Straightway, like a shot, I'm on me feet and I put me terrible face on. Like this!

SPRITE. That is a terrible face, is it, Knight?

KNIGHT. Of course it is. So, I'm standing there and I say to him: 'Halt. Give me thy name and wherefore comest thou hither.' That is the sort of thing you have to say. Then he says something technical to the effect that Our Lady is a scrubber... and I say: 'False Knight, thou liest', whereat I throw me glove down... (*Tugs frantically at his sleeve.*) like this... (*Triumphantly.*) and I say: 'Knight, I defy thee!' Then... Here, listen...

Perhaps he has noticed that the SPRITE *appears to have lost interest, since she is humming or combing her bright tresses or doing other spritely things.*

Anyway. You and me, we belong to different worlds. I mean, what'd it look like, a service conducted by a sea lion and you being given away by a crab. Do you, Sir, take this Water Sprite... etc. It wouldn't be right.

SPRITE. What is 'right'?

KNIGHT. There you go, you see. That's all technical as well. I mean, if you got no idea of laughing or suffering... You sure you never laughed at anything?

SPRITE. Never.

KNIGHT. Cor! Takes a bit of swallowing. Never been amused at nothing?

SPRITE. I don't think so.

KNIGHT. Well, what's the point of being alive at all, then?

SPRITE. That is what I want to find out.

KNIGHT. Mmmm. (*Pause, thinks.*) Listen. Suppose I was to tell you something very hilarious, very amusing, and suppose you was seized with the humour of it and before you could stop yourself you had burst out into a fit of laughing... well, then... as I see it, there'd be no need to actually go to the lengths of actually getting married! Do you see my plan?

SPRITE. Yes.

KNIGHT. Right. Right. Well. Now. Just set yourself... no... What you have to do is to completely relax... get yourself comfortable... sort of... yea... sort of like that... only... right... right... cor... This is hopeless... I mean, you sitting there with your big, tragic eyes staring at me... I mean... Right. Now then... er, wait a minute... Now, how does it go... Oh, yes... There was this man, see, and he had this dog... hee, hee, hee... oh, God... Well, there they are, oh, my God... the two o' them in this tavern and the owner of the tavern says to this man... No, I lie... No, it's the man says to the owner of the tavern, 'Hast thou any tallow candles, for the night is dark and I have far to go'... 'No,' quoth the owner of the tavern... 'I am all out of them. But...' says he, 'There be a tallow-candle maker a few rods and perches south of here.' 'Right,' says the man, and turning to the dog he says, 'Off thou goest, Towser, and get me a few dozen candles,' and he hands the dog a groat and says, 'And mind what thou doest with the change.' 'Here,' says the taverner, 'what art thou up to?' 'Have no fear, good taverner,' says the man. 'This is a very bright dog.' So off trots the dog, see, and they settle down to wait its return. Well, they wait and they wait and they wait and soon it's as black as a monkey's... well, very dark, anyway, and the taverner says, 'Looks like thy dog hast gone for ye Burton.' And he laughs. 'Yea. Verily,' says the man, 'and when I catch up with that wight I will have something to say unto him.' So off go the taverner and this man to find out what happened to the dog

and... well... after a bit of shrieking and crying and callin'
out what should they see but the dog havin' it off with a lady
dog... see... well... hee, hee, hee... oh, God... So, anyway,
the man says to the dog, 'Thou caitiff, thou hast never done
this before!' 'Nay, verily,' replies the dog, 'but then I have
never had the money before!!' See... hee, hee, hee, the dog
says, I have never... had the money... before. Never... You
don't get it, do you?

SPRITE. I understand the story, Knight. The man has kept the
dog in penury and so the dog was unable to pay for the
sexual favours of his own female kind. It is a very sad story.
Is that what humans would think?

KNIGHT. Well...

SPRITE. I ask because I notice you doing the 'ha, ha, ha' which
humans do so much when they perceive the sadness of
others, as they do the 'boo-hoo-hoo' when they are sad themselves. All this I will learn, I suppose, when I become
human.

KNIGHT. No, no, no. (*In despair.*) You won't *learn*. Being
human is being vulnerable and laughing and crying... it's
'oh, oh, oh', not 'boo-hoo' or 'ha, ha'... What it is... it's
pain, being born, not living very long, seeing death and
suffering death, and laughing and being brief to see the
world and the things in it... Oh, dear. I'm a soft white thing
that bleeds, my dear, nothing admirable or to be pursued, and
I put this iron casing round myself because inside it's soft
and white and vulnerable and fearful and ready to live or to
die... to be sliced, to be chopped off... and to laugh a bit...
It's all complicated, being human is, and not something you
learn... It's a bloody gift we was born to and given by some
cruel being who loves us, *inexplicably*, as my wise old dad
used to say... and it's sometimes being a genius with the
suffering and the good bits, being human and keeping to the
line and the rules... and... and... all that... and this... Me.
Humanity. That's what we are.

He takes off his helmet and shows her the sorry picture.

A ruin, my dear, a sort of smiling ruin. You see.

SPRITE. I would like to know all these things. They are all things I would like to know. When we are... born... the sea washes our eyes and we feel the sea around us and the creatures of the sea and swim through caverns of green water, Knight, and break from the sea to the air and the sky is blue, Knight, and the wind is blowing... and we are here for ever and we do not know why.

KNIGHT. Ah.

SPRITE. We are elemental, Knight, like the sand and the sea and the sky. We have eyes and ears and we feel but we are like the elements perceiving... Knight... We have only one desire... to care that we are alive... and I have heard it said we need death... mortality... to do that, Knight.

KNIGHT. Yer, it's a problem all right.

SPRITE. Yes.

KNIGHT. Ho-hum. Here, did I ever tell you about a friend o' mine?

SPRITE. 'Friend'?

KNIGHT. Er... em...well, like, somebody I knew... somebody I... er... *cared* about. Now he was a caring man... a careless sort of caring man... he was... great one for living... threw himself at it... but very... honourable... with it... he was. Very. I'm not anybody, you see. Worked meself up, I did, to where I am now. That, in a nutshell, is the meaning of my life... Not that I'm anybody now... because I have not got the talent... the grace for that... no, but, I've worked my way up from a scullion, really, to where I can take a stand, do things that have a touch of... nobility, you see... offer meself against... against... and stand... and not go back... and resist... and... all that... But my friend, he was born to it, water off a duck's back was grace and nobility to him. He was such a person, my dear, made me respect the stuff we was made of, this... this stuff. (*Pinching it*.) Anyway, one day, he and me was out on a perilous mission and he comes up against this giant of a being, a veritable giant of a being... and he's defending himself very stoutly but this giant has arms like... like... huge columns of stone, they were, and a sword this big, I swear, and so sharp and glittering, blinding ye with the swings, and he swings and he swings... and all the glories of my friend are of no avail. Well, I'm pretty encompassed myself with this other second-rate giant... giantess, actually... grey, greasy hair she had and she's big enough for three... and then this other giant gives this huge swipe and I sees... I sees... I sees my friend's arm is all sliced off, neat as you please, all sliced off... so I looks at him... and he nods... and there's a dark look on his face... and he falls... I tell you, miss, I would not have been in his mind at that moment for all the glory and the greatness in the whole world... For there he was... and he died... and he was a man of grace and light... and he had this expression on his face... that's what he had. This expression.

For some time now the SPRITE *has been distracted for some reason.*

SPRITE. Knight!

KNIGHT. Not for all the tea in Cathay. No.

SPRITE. Knight!

KNIGHT. Clean as a whistle. Lying there. The arm. And his armpit was all red.

SPRITE. I hear a roaring, Knight.

KNIGHT. What's that, my dear?

SPRITE. I think it be a dragon.

KNIGHT (*not taking this inexpert opinion seriously but going through the motions*). Hah! A dragon, eh?

SPRITE. I think it be so.

KNIGHT. Ah, well, if it be a dragon... er... (*He consults his book.*) Dragons, dragon... let's... d – r... agon... uhuh... 'a dragon being perceived...'

SPRITE. It is very adjacent.

KNIGHT. Adjacent, eh? I can't hear nothing. Mind you, that's no criterion, what with all this headgear and that and the batterin' it's had, my hearing int all that much nowadays. Roaring, you say?

Whether there be the occasional roar here is left to taste.

SPRITE. Oh, yes.

KNIGHT. Well... mmm... actually, to be quite frank, if it is a dragon, and I am not saying it ain't, I, for one, will be very surprised. I mean, I know I told you all that stuff about maidens and that and I do know for a fact that rumour has it that there used to be quite a lot of these dragon things hanging around, time of Canute and that, you could hardly avoid bumping into a dragon or two. But things is all different now. I mean, these are modern times, see what I mean, all that stuff about dragons and that, it's all in the past now. Modern technology being what it is, cannons, gunpowder, the new spill-bright sword, lightweight maces, I mean, your dragon nowadays would not stand a cat in hell's chance, if you'll pardon the expression, miss.

SPRITE. Nevertheless, the roaring I hear, Knight, is undoubtedly that made by a rampant dragon. I know these things. I have been many years in the world.

KNIGHT. Yea, well, like I say... I'll just climb up 'ere and have a peek, see what's goin' on. Could be some kind of rural creature, I suppose... No, can't see a dicky bird... can't... 'Ere, half a mo... What's tha... Blast these non-stick visors... There is something hoving up, certainly... 'Ere, miss, lend's your eyes for a minute, will ye, mine has gone off a bit... There. See. Now... what is that?

SPRITE (*as calm as a cucumber*). It is a dragon, Knight.

KNIGHT. Mmmm. Well, that's as maybe. Just as well to check, isn't it? Hang on. (*He thumbs through his little red book again.*) Does it have horns?

SPRITE. No.

KNIGHT. Well, that's right enough. If it had had horns... What colour is it?

SPRITE. Green, of course. It is all green, Knight. Except for its eyes.

KNIGHT. Which are what?

SPRITE. Very red.

KNIGHT. Very red. Ho-hum. La-de-da and all that. The evidence is piling up and all that. There wouldn't, by any chance, be a sort of haze hanging over it… like what you'd expect if a creature'd been belchin' out huge gobbets of flame and that…?

SPRITE. Yes, there is an haze. A great haze.

KNIGHT. A great haze! God Almighty! That's it, then. Bloody great big colossal dragon hoving up and I would have to be right in the monster's path, so to speak. Here, you don't think, do you, if we was to stay low and keep very still and quiet he might go past.

SPRITE. He might.

KNIGHT. No chance. Dragons have a nose for knights. He is probably sniffing the air now, the great, green, bloody idiot. 'Mmm,' he says, 'munch, munch,' he says. Just my luck. Ten years ago I might've stood a chance but I'm getting on, my dear, a few months now I'm up for retirement, get me staff and me robe and me chimney corner, a game o' draughts and nod away the hours… aaaah!

SPRITE. He is getting very close, Knight. What will you do?

KNIGHT. Do? You may well ask, madam. What can I do? Go forth. That is what I can do. Mount me old crippled nag and with a cry of 'Honour, honour and My Lady' go and get the living daylights belted out of me, that is what I gotta do.

SPRITE. You will kill him, Knight?

KNIGHT. Oh, yes. One blow and he's had it. Ah, this is it, Sir Lancelot. This is your lot, all right. I'm sorry we never got round to getting married, miss… But, anyway, it'd never have worked out. And… er… if I was you, miss, while 'e's roaring and munching and devouring my… er… whatsits… you would be well advised to move on.

SPRITE. No, thank you. I shall stay. He will not harm me. His fire will not burn my water.

KNIGHT. Ah, good for you, then, good for you. Well, there he is. I defy thee, monster. (*Shakes a wavering weapon.*) Now, where's that book? Damn!

Finds it hard to see what page it is and reluctantly draws out a pair of medieval spectacles which he puts on his nose, giving the SPRITE *an apologetic glance as to say 'Well, now you know it all.' Then he moves off in the direction of his foe, and then, before going off to mortal combat, reads from the text.*

'Lady, I go forth to encounter this fell dragon. Peradventure I shall be slain but be the cause just and my arm strong in that cause I shall prevail. Remember me.' Right. That's that bit. (*He pauses.*) Right. I shall prevail. Goodbye.

SPRITE. Goodbye, Knight.

He exits, and we now hear him calling:

KNIGHT. Dragon, I charge thee to submit to my knightly will. Have at thee now.

A roar. Clash of arms, roaring, yelling and then silence. The SPRITE *hums and does her spritely thing. A looking glass, maybe. She may even rise to do a few graceful dance steps. Then the* KNIGHT *returns. Either he is carrying, or dragging, with some difficulty, on a long length of rope, perhaps, the wonderful fierce green head of the dragon. (Either that or while he is off there is silence and then a mighty roar or just silence and then he comes back in, etc. I prefer the roaring thing myself.)*

I did it!! I did it!! I slew him. With one stroke. One bloody stroke. Lady, I lay this monster's head at thy feet and I lay this proud sword at thy feet and I tell thee, lady, all is secure… may God… defend… the… right.

He groans, staggers and falls over and away from the SPRITE, *who is left with the head.*

SPRITE. Alas, alas…

KNIGHT. No, no… it's all right. Don't you grieve. Don't you fret. It's all right.

The SPRITE *cradles the head on her lap and fondles it.*

SPRITE. Alas, alas, poor creature, poor beautiful creature!

KNIGHT. No, listen, I don't want you to fret. I mean, I did, after all, slay a dragon and there's not many can say that... I'm going out when I'm on top, see... miss... miss...

SPRITE. Oh, sadness, that this death should be my cause.

KNIGHT. Yea, well, it is a bit sad, I suppose... Here... miss... can you hear me? I can't hardly hear meself!

SPRITE (*speaking of the dragon, but the* KNIGHT *still thinks she is fretting over him*). Eyes in death, lips in death.

KNIGHT. Yea, well, there's a spark or two left yet, you know. Miss, d'you hear... would you just find me book... find the bit where it goes on about knights what have been wounded... mortally wounded... even... and say what it says... will you... just that bit.

SPRITE. You were so strong and innocent and supernatural and belonged to the world who now are dead... dead... dead...

KNIGHT. Could ya... that bit... Ah, well, doesn't matter. Not your place, really... But I done it. I done it. There's probably not another dragon in all the ways of the world and I was the one that done it... And now it's all safe... all the damsels and the villeins... and their sheep and their goats and their children... all safe... no more dragons... Gone... Wish I coulda heard that bit, miss... that bit... 'And his eyes shall close in peace who has fought justly and well and has conquered and there shall be peace in his heart and he shall know peace...' Yea. That's it! 'For courage and truth and honour lived he and at the end was mourning and joy.' Yea, that is definitely it. A Water Sprite. Ha, ha. You have to laugh... ha, ha... you have to laugh.

SPRITE. Alas, alas!

KNIGHT. Here, you grieving, are you? Did I hear you grieving?

SPRITE. I grieve.

KNIGHT. Well, that's good then, you grieving, cos, you see, you grieving over me is just as good as laughing, see what I mean... I done it... the lot... You're human now, see, human.

SPRITE. Poor beast, poor, poor dumb beast. The human has killed you. That is what they do.

KNIGHT. Yea, human...

SPRITE. Knight, can you hear me... can you... You... you... you have killed him and now... no more... I hate you... I hate you... I hate you. (*She weeps and fondles the last dragon's head*.) Hate, hate, hate. I don't want to be human. I don't want to be human. Do you hear?

KNIGHT. Oh, yes. You're human now, see. Human.

So she weeps for it is –

The End.

RAMALLAH

David Greig

David Greig's award-winning work includes *Dunsinane* (Royal Shakespeare Company at Hampstead Theatre); *Midsummer* (with Gordon McIntyre; Traverse Theatre and Soho Theatre); *Creditors* (Donmar Warehouse and BAM); *Damascus* and *Miniskirts of Kabul* (Tricycle Theatre); *Brewers Fayre*, *Outlying Islands* and *Europe* (Traverse Theatre); *The American Pilot* (Royal Shakespeare Company, Soho Theatre and MTC); *Ramallah* (Royal Court Theatre); *Pyrenees* (Paines Plough) and *The Cosmonaut's Last Message to the Woman He Once Loved in the Former Soviet Union* (Donmar Warehouse). Adaptations include *The Bacchae* (Edinburgh International Festival and Lyric Theatre, Hammersmith); *Tintin in Tibet* (Barbican and The Playhouse); *When the Bulbul Stopped Singing* (Traverse Theatre); *Caligula* (Donmar Warehouse) and *Peter Pan* (National Theatre of Scotland and Barbican).

Ramallah was first performed as a rehearsed reading at the Royal Court Theatre, London, on 13 March 2004, with the following cast:

DANIEL	Daniel Evans
HELEN	Monica Dolan
Director	Ramin Gray

It received its first production at the Tron Theatre, Glasgow, as part of the triple bill *From the West Bank*, in May 2010.

Characters

DANIEL, *mid-thirties*

HELEN, *mid-thirties*

A late-summer evening.

A wooden kitchen table.

A blue-glass bowl full of plums.

Two empty wine glasses.

A bottle of red wine.

A small collection of plain polythene bags on the floor.

A man and woman, both in their early thirties.

DANIEL *and* HELEN.

DANIEL *pours the wine.*

HELEN   It's nice to have you back.

DANIEL   It's good to be –
    It's strange.

        He kisses her.

HELEN   You smell of cigarettes.

DANIEL   Yes. I know.

HELEN   Were you smoking?

DANIEL   Everyone smokes there. It's almost rude not to.
    And it was a tense environment.
    It's difficult to explain.
    I wanted to smoke.

HELEN   So you've started smoking.

DANIEL   I haven't started smoking.
    I smoked.
    There is a difference.

HELEN   You can't smoke in the house.

DANIEL   Of course not.

Something of a pause.

What do you think of the wine?

HELEN *tastes.*

HELEN   Mmm.

DANIEL   Good, isn't it?
            It's made by monks.
            I visited the vineyard.
            The vineyard is thousands of years old.
            Biblical.
            Hardly changed in a thousand years.

HELEN   You should call Sam, by the way.
            She left a message for you.
            I wonder if there's maybe a job.

DANIEL   Okay.
            I'll do it tomorrow.

HELEN   It's just we're getting close to the overdraft limit,
            Daniel.

DANIEL   Sure.

HELEN   We've been tightening the belt here while you've
            been gone.

DANIEL   Right.
            I'll call her.

Something of a pause.

It's surprisingly good, though, isn't it.
I don't know if there's anywhere here that stocks
   it.
There should be.
I think people would buy this.
Even it was just out of solidarity.

HELEN   It's nice to have a glass of wine in the evening.
            The children in bed.
            Just to sit.
            I haven't really been able to do that.

DANIEL   You've had your hands full.

HELEN   Yes.

Something of a pause.

Are you hungry?

DANIEL   A bit.

HELEN   I'll get some crisps.

DANIEL   No, wait... wait. I brought something back.

He looks in a polythene bag.

Cheese.
Feta.
Wait.
Paprika.
And olive oil.
Do we have pitta bread?

HELEN   No. I haven't been shopping. There wasn't time.

DANIEL   Do we have a lemon? We must have a lemon?

HELEN   I think so... somewhere.

DANIEL   Here we go.

He finds a lemon and a sharp knife.

You should have seen the lemons there.
We went to the fruit and vegetable market every
     day.
Just the colours were amazing.
Lemons and oranges and watermelons and...
     things.

He cuts the feta up.

I thought of you;
I thought that you would have taken photographs
     of the piles of fruit in the market.

He sprinkles some paprika over it.

Lemons the size of my fist and thick-skinned.
You could smell them from five yards away.
The citrus oils just hanging in the air.

He pours some olive oil over it.

Fruit everywhere.
Everybody has some kind of tree.
Tiny gardens. Window boxes.
Everybody growing something.

He squeezes some lemon juice over it.

Taste that.

HELEN *takes some.*

HELEN   Mmm.
            That's nice.

DANIEL   Isn't it?
            And of course
            you can just whip it up for a snack.
            And we would sit on the verandah in the evening.
            And the sun would be going down.
            Watch the kids on the waste ground throwing
                stones.
            And we'd talk through the ideas for the play.
            A couple of bottles of beer
            Perfect.

HELEN   It does sound idyllic –

DANIEL   One night. The family who lived opposite. They
            were just sitting out in the road. Sitting on the
            pavement taking the air. They invited us to
            join them. The man spoke English. His father
            was there. And his mother. And his wife. And
            there were about five kids.

HELEN   That's typical, isn't it. Wouldn't happen here.

DANIEL   No. No. Exactly.
            The wife brought out all sorts of food, and coffee.
            And we talked to the children.

We were up on a hill, we had a view over the city.
The grandmother pointed towards the west.
Towards the coast.
That's where she was from.
The son translated her story.
Everybody has a story, you know, everybody
    makes sure you hear their story. You get used
    to it. You listen and nod. What can you say?
She kept pointing out towards the coast.

Something of a pause.

HELEN   These plums are from our garden.

DANIEL   Are they?

HELEN   It's been a really good year this year.

    DANIEL *takes one.*

DANIEL   They're okay. Aren't they.

HELEN   The children and I harvested them.
    I took the stepladders out from the shed.
    Johnny harvested all the low-down plums.
    Sarah climbed up the ladder. She harvested all the
        high-up plums.
    I harvested all the plums in the middle.

DANIEL   It sounds like fun.

HELEN   It was fun.

    Something of a pause.

    The kids will be excited to see you.

DANIEL   I'm excited to see them.

HELEN   Have you been into the bedroom? I think they're
        asleep.

DANIEL   No.
    I will.
    I didn't want to wake them.
    Let's just…

HELEN	Okay.
	Something of a pause.
	Sarah's been wetting the bed.
DANIEL	Oh. I thought she'd stopped doing that.
HELEN	Well, she started again.
DANIEL	Do you know why?
HELEN	I think it's probably the disruption. You being away.
DANIEL	I suppose.
HELEN	She listens to the radio at breakfast. I forget that it's on. And I wonder if she didn't hear a few things. Because I was always noticing – if it was in the news.
DANIEL	Oh.
HELEN	She asked me if Ramallah was the place where you were.
DANIEL	What did you say?
HELEN	I said yes.
DANIEL	And what did she say?
HELEN	She said 'I thought so.'
DANIEL	Did she say anything else?
HELEN	I didn't want to press her.
DANIEL	She could have heard anything.
HELEN	That's what I thought.
	Something of a pause.
DANIEL	She must have been worried.
HELEN	I think so. I tried to speak to her about it but she wouldn't let me.

DANIEL   Poor thing.

Something of a pause.

One day we went to visit a children's theatre
company. They had built their own theatre,
converted it from a garage or something.
They put on shows for children there. But
unfortunately they built their theatre opposite
a settlement so now it's on the front line.
Every night there's shooting back and forth. I
saw it. The place is covered in bullet holes.
And then one night it was hit by a tank shell.
There was a show going on at the time. They
told us how they had to evacuate the children
in small groups with the tank firing away.
You'd think it was a bit much – firing a tank
shell at a children's theatre – you'd think they
wouldn't do that. But I saw the place where
the shell knocked through the wall.

Something of a pause.

Anyway, they performed a show, especially for us,
in the rubble of their theatre.

Something of a pause.

My palms were sweating all the way through the
show.
I just wanted to get the fuck out.
Because I didn't want to die.

Something of a pause.

They said you never get used to the feeling.

HELEN   You said you would be careful, Daniel.

DANIEL   I was careful.

HELEN   But you went to this... 'front line'.

DANIEL   I was exaggerating.

HELEN   Okay.

DANIEL   Besides, I couldn't not go.
          I couldn't refuse to see their fucking show.

HELEN   It's okay. I understand.

DANIEL   Jesus.
          These people are getting the shit kicked out of
              them every fucking day.
          And they have to carry on.
          I'm a tourist. I can go home.
          Right now, Helen.
          Right at this very moment they are afraid.
          Their kids are afraid.
          The least I can do is piss myself for half an hour
              on their behalf.
          Get a flavour of things.

HELEN   I think you're overreacting, Daniel.

DANIEL   I'm sorry.
          You're right. I'm overreacting.

HELEN   I was worried about you.
          That's all.

DANIEL   Okay. I know.

HELEN   But you're back now.

DANIEL   I tell you what.
          I'm just – it's the nicotine withdrawal.
          I'm grumpy.
          That's what it is.

HELEN   Have a cigarette if you want.
          I don't mind.

DANIEL   No.
          That's it.
          Finished with.

HELEN   It'll take a bit of getting used to.
          Readjusting to having you back.

DANIEL   Yeah.

HELEN   We've got used to being on our own.

DANIEL   Yeah.

HELEN   And now you're back.

          Something of a pause.

DANIEL   Tonight,
          I got off the train, and the air smelt familiar,
          Because of the sea
          And I walked down the brae from the station,
          The pink valerian is in flower, growing out of the
               walls.
          The sun was going down over the harbour
          My bag was heavy.
          I thought
          I'm coming home.
          And...
          I realised – you realise – one realises...
          How lucky one is – I realised how lucky I am –
          We are.
          We are.

54% ACRYLIC

David Harrower

David Harrower is an internationally acclaimed playwright. Previous work includes *Knives in Hens* (Traverse Theatre and Bush Theatre); *Kill the Old Torture Their Young*, *Dark Earth* (Traverse Theatre); *The Chrysalids* (NT Connections); *Presence* (Royal Court Theatre); *Blackbird* (Edinburgh International Festival, West End, Manhattan Theatre Club and Sydney Theatre Company); *365* (National Theatre of Scotland). Adaptations include *Six Characters in Search of an Author*, *The Good Soul of Szechuan* and *Sweet Nothings,* a version of Schnitzler's *Liebelei* (Young Vic Theatre); *Woyzeck* (Edinburgh Lyceum Theatre); *Ivanov*, *Tales from the Vienna Woods* (Royal National Theatre); *The Girl on the Sofa* (Edinburgh International Festival and the Schaubuhne, Berlin); *Mary Stuart* (National Theatre of Scotland).

54% Acrylic was first broadcast on BBC Radio 4 on 8 July 1998, with the following cast:

GERRY   James Cosmo
MARION   Tracy Wiles
SUPERVISOR   Matthew Zajac

Director   Claire Grove

Characters

GERRY

MARION

SECURITY SUPERVISOR

A large department store.

GERRY. I watched her. She came in. I watched her come in and she went straight to the escalator. She was... nineteen... A girl. A woman... A girl. And she was wearing a blue jacket. She was nineteen, twenty, twenty-one. About that. Blue jacket and white jeans. And white trainers. White trainers that were dirty, that were scuffed.

She went to the escalator and she looked to me like she knew what she was there for. I think she knew what it was she wanted. She knew where it was.

And her hair was up. She'd tied it up like a lot of them... You see a lot of them wearing it like it now. The girls. Young ones. They tie it up... tie it back.

MARION. They weren't where they were before. Everything was moved around again. It's always happening in the big stores. I don't know why they do it – it's annoying. Is it 'cause there's nothing else to do and they have to find the assistants something to do?

I found them eventually. They'd shifted them to a corner. All the reds had gone. There was only greens left – three left in the green. I couldn't believe it. Two days ago, Wednesday, they'd had six or seven reds. Now they'd all gone. That's what I went in for, that dress, to have a look at it again. I'd tried it on, the red – it had these thin, thin shoulder straps – and it looked beautiful. I thought it looked beautiful on me.

The green was a dark green; bottle green. Green's not a colour I wear much – I thought it always made me look too pale, my skin. It was the shape of the dress I really liked, the length of it. I kept looking at it, trying to imagine it on me and I thought I might as well try it on. They had two of them in size ten, which is my size. I still had half an hour before I started back at my work.

GERRY. I was talking to… Who was I talking to? Someone. A
colleague. One of the women there. I talk to a whole lot of
people in a day, but the ones on the ground floor, the people, I
don't know as many as I used to. They change them all the
time nowadays. There's always new faces I never know the
names of. I talk to whoever's behind the counters or if there's
someone on the floor, maybe arranging stock. There's always
a joke or a story or… about the customers that've come in the
store or one of the staff or the managers; our supervisors.
Something's always happening somewhere in the store. A
child's got themselves lost. Women faint. People are sick.

When I say – I don't mean conversations, not a long
conversation. We're working so we can't talk long. It
wouldn't look right.

MARION. It was the same girl that's always there that was
outside the changing room. She recognised me, I could see it,
but her face stayed the same. She always looked at me the
same. Like I should dress up just to go in there. I should apologise just for being there. Her hair looked brilliant. Expensive. And she'd been on a sunbed. People would say if they
saw her on the street that she was beautiful, I think. They'd –
a lot of people would turn their heads as she passed. She
must've been used to that. I had the size ten and a size twelve,
in case. I showed them to her and said two and she gave me a
black plastic thing. I asked if she'd any reds left. She said if
there's none there, if there's none on the rail then no, no, we
haven't, sorry. And the way she said sorry, I could've hit her.

GERRY. It might've been her face. It could've been something
about her face – and the way she came in and walked straight
to the escalator, without being interested in anything else.
That could've been it. Most of them when they come in,
they've planned the whole thing ahead.

We can usually tell with people. We just know. Because you
learn to tell these things. Over time we learn to spot them –
characteristics. And some of them, some of them just give
themselves away. They don't even know they're doing it.
They could just as well come in with a white bag with 'swag'
written on it. With those people, we just know.

MARION. What was it? Gerry…? About me?

I know your name. You told me your name. Tell me…
Gerry? What was it?

GERRY. It can be anything.

MARION. What…?

My face? Was it my face?

GERRY. It…

MARION *laughs*.

MARION. Was it written all over my face?

GERRY. No. It's… I got a sense…

Maybe it was. Maybe it was your face when I saw it, yes.
The way you were. The way you were acting. It can be a
very simple thing. It needs to only be a small thing.

Pause.

MARION. Where were you?

GERRY. Where was I? On the ground floor.

MARION. When I came in…

GERRY. That was my floor. I…

MARION. Your floor?

GERRY. The floor I was covering. My floor. We're each
responsible for a floor. We get allocated a floor. I was
standing at the doors. No, I was…

MARION. And you saw me…

GERRY. I was watching you. I was further in. I saw you. I was
talking to one of the women that works there on the ground.

MARION. Yes. My face…

GERRY. Or something about you.

MARION. That you thought – her.

GERRY. Yes.

It could've been what she, the girl, was wearing, the blue
jacket she was wearing that was... it – I didn't get a good
enough look – it was zipped up or... or unzipped. There was
sunshine outside on the street. The sun was bright. It was
warm. It was shining in the glass of the doors. It was maybe
that. It was maybe that her jacket was zipped up.

Pause.

MARION. I looked at myself in the mirror for ages in the size
ten. It showed off a lot of me. I could see my shoulders bare.
I didn't mind the colour of it, the green, now. I liked it on
me. I didn't think I would but I did. There were other mirrors
so you could see it from the back and even from the back it
looked good. I was thinking where I'd wear it, where out I'd
wear it. And how many times. You wouldn't see it in the pub.
It was for a party or a... some special occasion. It was a
dress people'd remember. They'd look at me in it and maybe
they would... I don't know, they'd... think things about me.
They'd think I was such-and-such a person. But that's alright
just for a night. I told myself buy it, just buy it, you deserve
it. I had the money – fifty quid – but I'd have nothing left for
the weekend. I didn't get paid for another two weeks. I
thought I'd leave it for just now. I might see something
somewhere else. And I could always come back for it. I'm in
town every day, the centre of town, so I could always go
back and get it. I didn't even think.

GERRY. About what?

MARION. They'd have people like you. I should've thought.

GERRY. Like me?

MARION. Detectives. Store detectives.

GERRY. You shouldn't think about me. It shouldn't even cross
your mind. Even if you look for me, you shouldn't be able to
spot me. I should be invisible. In the background. In my
jeans and my jacket, every day, carrying a plastic bag or an
umbrella or... like any other customer, you see.

MARION. It sounds, doesn't it? – 'detective' – sounds so...

GERRY. What? That's what I do. I look for clues. I am a detective. I'm good at my job. I've been doing it for a lot of years. I'm good at what I do.

Escalator. GERRY *radios* SECURITY SUPERVISOR.

Delta Three calling HQ, come in, please...

Delta Three calling HQ...

Pause.

SUPERVISOR. What is it, Delta Three?

GERRY. I think I've got a sighting, HQ. She's a...

SUPERVISOR. Confirm your position for me first, will you, Delta Three?

GERRY. I'm on the escalator, HQ, going up to first.

SUPERVISOR. First?

GERRY. Roger.

SUPERVISOR. You're third floor, Delta Three, what're you doing on first?

GERRY. I was on ground, HQ. I'm now on first. I'm covering. Delta One and Two are on lunch.

SUPERVISOR. Of course they are. Of course they are.

Pause.

GERRY. I followed her up from ground. (*Pause.*) Do you want me to stay here, HQ...?

SUPERVISOR. I suppose so, Delta Three. You're the only one I've got left. Where are you on first?

GERRY. To the left of the escalator.

Pause.

SUPERVISOR. I've got you. Delta Three, I can see you now. So it's just you and me. Where is she then? Give me a position.

Pause.

GERRY. I've lost her just for the moment.

I think she's still on first.

SUPERVISOR. First floor is women's wear. Would you say she was a woman? How closely did you look, Delta Three?

Pause.

GERRY. She's wearing blue jacket, white jeans, white trainers. She's about nineteen, twenty.

SUPERVISOR. Oh, same year you were born, Delta Three... Blue jacket, white jeans... Back with you in a moment, Delta Three. Don't go anywhere. Over and out.

MARION. Outside the girl said – and she was smiling now like she'd just told a joke – said are you taking it? Or... no – I'll put it back for you. I told her I'd put it back and she smiled some more and shook her head. They get discounts on clothes for working in there, I know that. They can buy as many clothes as they want.

GERRY. The moment a person enters the store they become a potential thief. For us. The supervisor's always stressing that. Because we have nothing else to help us. We have only our intuition to act on. Or hunches. Simple hunches. We have to be able to second-guess them.

He's upstairs – the security supervisor – at the top of the building in a room where they've got all the screens. The security screens. And that enables him to see everything that's going on, in any part of the store.

MARION. I put the dresses back on the rail. I was ready to leave. There was another shop I had time to look in. I touched the dress again; I felt it. Today was Friday. Then Saturday. Then Saturday night. I didn't know where I was going yet, a club or... but it'd be somewhere. And I'd be excited. And wanting to have a good time. I thought: I'm sick of wearing jeans all the time. People always see me in jeans. I want to be in something different. Nobody was around me. Nobody was near me. I looked up to see where the camera was on the ceiling but there was nothing there. The dress was dark green. There was so little of it. For fifty pounds.

She unzips her jacket, takes dress off the hanger, pushes the
dress into her jacket, zips it up.

GERRY. When we suspect a customer, when we have a suspect
in the store, what we have to then do is get ourselves into a
position where we can observe that person, where we can
watch them without them, of course, being aware that they
are being watched. So that if – or when – an item is then
stolen by them, this will be seen either by the detective themselves on the floor or recorded by the security cameras. The
suspect is then followed at a suitable distance until they
make a move towards an exit. We can do nothing up till this
point. We wait. Strictly speaking, they are still, by law, customers. It is only when the suspect has passed the last till and
it is evident they have no intention of paying for the item that
we can move in on them. We apprehend ninety to ninety-five
per cent of them that way. At or just outside the front doors.

SUPERVISOR. Blue jacket, Delta Three, there's a blue jacket
white jeans on your far left. Eleven o'clock. Far corner.

GERRY. Roger. Heading there now, HQ.

SUPERVISOR. She's just looking, Delta Three. She's not doing
anything so far.

MARION. I walked away and stood somewhere else. I pretended to look at another dress. I couldn't believe I'd... No, I
could, I could. It was... there. I could feel it in my jacket
next to me. I had it there. I couldn't go back – that was the
other thing. I knew I couldn't put it back. 'Cause I'd done it
so quickly and so... so... neatly it felt... awkward to un...
– to pull it back out, let it drop on the floor or whatever,
leave it lying there on the floor of the shop in a heap.

GERRY. There's three of us for the whole store and we each
have a floor each. I've got the third floor – household items,
crockery, furniture, stuff like that. I've been here the longest
of them so I know the procedures inside out. I know what
can happen. People are incredible. They'll take your breath
away what they can do. Anything that's not nailed down
twice they'll steal. We watch them upstairs sometimes on the
security screens – the supervisor plays the recording and

we… Well, we're used to it, we… But it's the, the, the
desperation and the… well – stupidity. The – foolishness.
Foolhardy, is it? It's incredible to watch these people. When
they believe they're all alone, when they are past caring
even, and what they will just grab at, what they will reach
out for and stuff into their bags or jackets or down into their
trousers.

SUPERVISOR. C'mon, Delta Three, move it. She could've had
half the shop by now if she wanted.

Delta Three, was her jack – ? She's moving now. She's
moving, she's moving, Delta Three, she's… coming at you.
Stop right there. She's coming right at you.

MARION. That was you…

GERRY. You were ahead of me.

MARION. Walking towards you. (*Laughs.*) That was you. In
ladies underwear.

GERRY. The only man there. Alone.

MARION. I saw your face. Very quickly. Not your eyes. You
turned away.

GERRY. I was looking for black underwear.

MARION. And I didn't… I didn't even think.

GERRY. I tried to look normal. There was nothing odd about
me being there.

MARION. No. No, I thought…

GERRY. What?

MARION. That you were a… man – a poor man on, yes, on his
own there. A man who looked lost. Embarrassed. Who had
come in wanting to buy underwear for a surprise for his…
her birthday… his girlfriend… or just as a surprise 'cause he
loved her, his girlfriend or his wife, his… And who had been
caught by another woman. Nearly caught. Because you
turned away. You turned your eyes away.

GERRY. Because men buy, don't they? Buy women, they
always buy women black underwear, not white. Women buy

white underwear for thernselves. Men buy black – or red.
Or... or... They do buy white, of course they do, white sus-
penders, white bras but I could only think black. The sexy
stuff. That's what I thought.

MARION. I walked past you, didn't I? I walked right past you.
I didn't suspect a thing.

Pause.

GERRY. From time to time we'll have to go onto another floor, a
floor that's not ours, following a suspect. And that can be... it
can be say the women's wear department or... towels and
linen, say, or... baby clothes – baby clothes and it can look
odd, me, a man, being there on my own. We have to be
careful. We have to watch ourselves. Because we can always
– it's very easy to overstep the mark. We can make it look too
obvious what we're doing. They're not dummies, a lot of
them. They're not stupid. They can sense us, who we are, as
much as we sense them. I've seen it happen. Something will
click. Nothing will register but they'll have clicked and they'll
know what we are. And they'll move somewhere else or bend
down behind a stand and get rid of... dump whatever they
have on them. This's of course in a way what we're there for.
We've prevented the crime. We've prevented a theft from
taking place. But not in a manner that satisfies us. We would
rather see a conviction or fine or at least a verbal warning from
the police because without any of those things it'll only be a
matter of time before that person is out robbing again. Maybe
not in our store but in any of the other ones nearby.

SUPERVISOR (*whispering*). Delta Three...?

GERRY. Roger, HQ.

SUPERVISOR. Don't turn round. Stay as you are.

Beautiful, isn't it? That black underwear you're looking at.
You should buy some for your wife.

GERRY. Where is she?

SUPERVISOR. She's near the top of the escalator. She hasn't
gone down yet.

She was right on top of you.

GERRY. She saw me, did she?

SUPERVISOR. She didn't blink an eye, Delta Three. You're a magician. No, no, better, better, you are an iguana. An iguana, Delta Three. You were incredible. She thought you were buying a... surprise for your bloody girlfriend or something. And so did I, Delta Three, so did I. I'm glad we've got that on camera. I'll have to play that back later on for you. And the others. Delta One and Two have got to see that.

Was her jacket zipped up when she came in, Delta Three, do you know?

Pause.

GERRY. I don't know. I can't say.

SUPERVISOR. Or unzipped...

GERRY. I can't remember, HQ. I didn't get a good look.

SUPERVISOR. Okay, Delta Three, just wondering.

Pause.

MARION. The escalator was four or five steps away. It was right there, going down. I could feel the hum of it through the wooden floor. I only had to stand on it. If I stood on it I couldn't go back.

I was standing at a display of... socks or something. I looked over it and saw the changing-room girl. Saw her sulky face. She was beautiful-looking but she hadn't seen a thing. I thought: her haircut must've cost more than the dress. A woman, middle-aged maybe, was asking her a question but they must've had whatever it was 'cause she had to take her to it. She wasn't happy. She looked bored out her skull. It was almost funny. All the make-up and the tight clothes and she had to stand and listen to that woman wanting whatever it was. And I was going. I was leaving.

Pause.

SUPERVISOR. She's gone down, Delta Three. She's going down to ground.

GERRY. Roger, HQ.

SUPERVISOR. But, no...

GERRY. No?

SUPERVISOR. You see, I can't decide...

GERRY. Can't decide what?

SUPERVISOR. Can you see her?

GERRY. Roger.

SUPERVISOR. Jesus, she's stopped again... She's stopped at the bottom.

GERRY. I can see her.

SUPERVISOR. Is she only shopping? Do we think? I'm not sure. I don't know. We'll have to see what she does.

Careful now. Don't let her see you again.

Not much of a looker, is she, Delta Three? Could you not have done better than her? Why are they never slender young beauties with long, long legs, hmm?

Pause.

MARION. It was the doors.

GERRY. Why you stopped...

MARION. Yes, they were... it was the glass. The sun was coming through, shining through the glass.

GERRY. Your back was to me. I was behind you.

MARION. I couldn't go through them.

GERRY. I walked past you. I couldn't look.

MARION. The sun was on the doors. They were too bright. I thought for, I don't know why, I'd be caught in that brightness. I would be seen.

There was umbrellas there, near to me. I went to them.

GERRY. I had to look like I was leaving. In case she made a connection. I stopped at a perfume counter again. The woman behind it smiled at me but she knew not to speak.

They know when we're working. I pointed at a bottle and she brought it out from the glass counter and pretended to show it to me.

I had to wait. She could still come. She was behind me somewhere.

MARION. People were outside. They were on the street outside. I could see them through the doors.

The umbrellas were all colours. I tried to pick one I wanted.

I had to get there. I wanted to get to those people walking past outside. But not through the doors.

SUPERVISOR. Delta Three, she's off again...Where? Not to you. She's...Yes. Side exit. Thought so. She's going for the side exit.

GERRY. Roger, HQ.

SUPERVISOR. But I'm not convinced, Delta Three.

GERRY. You're not what?

SUPERVISOR. Convinced. She's taking too much time. To be honest, I think you should just drop her.

GERRY. HQ, she's been in the store less than five minutes...

SUPERVISOR. I don't know...

GERRY. I want to go with her.

SUPERVISOR. Do you?

GERRY. I'm sure of her.

SUPERVISOR. You're sure of this one?

GERRY. Yes.

SUPERVISOR. Are you sure?

GERRY. Let me go with her, HQ. I'm almost there now.

Pause.

SUPERVISOR. She's at the side exit now. I can see her. She's opening the door. Go on then, Delta Three. If you think you have to. Go after her.

GERRY. Roger, HQ.

SUPERVISOR. Maybe the fresh air will do you good.

Pause.

MARION. Nobody came to me. Nobody even looked at me.
There was one door and I pushed it open. I pushed on the
glass. I held my breath and walked out. There was nobody.
I knew there wouldn't be. I knew I was out. I looked back
quickly for a second, at the door behind me, ready to run.
Or – would I run? 'Cause I didn't think I would run. Where
would I run to? Away…? It was warm outside. I had my
jacket on. I think I wouldn't have run anywhere. I wouldn't
have got far. Even with my trainers on. I went along the
side of the store, past the windows there and my reflection
which I looked at but I saw nothing. No sign of a dress. I
was so, so happy suddenly. I was outside. It was like
walking in a different world all of a sudden. I came onto
the pedestrian precinct, and round to where the front doors
were. I looked in and they were all in there, all the people
who worked in the shop, they were all still in there and
none of them would ever find out what happened. They'd
never know what I did.

GERRY. When we do stop them, we ask them to come with us
up to the supervisor's office, we take them up there and the
supervisor will phone the police from there. They go with us
usually without much trouble, but sometimes, yes, they'll be
at it and refuse to, start shouting or resisting, thinking if
they embarrass us we'll let them go but we always, with
help, eventually get them up to the room and then we can
search them. We say we have reason to believe they've
stolen from the store, etc. etc…. will they submit to a search
and so on…

If we find a stolen item that's fine, everyone's happy. We
have done the job we're paid to do. If we don't, if we
– 'cause there's times we can be mistaken – if we find
nothing then, then we can have a problem. It's, legally,
within their legal rights to press charges against us. For… for
– it's called defamation of character. I don't know how. But
they can get us for that. Or even harassment, even. We lay

one finger on them and we're wrong about it, they can bring that against us. So we have to be convinced about what we're doing. It's happened to me – it happens to us all – three or four times last year, where I got it wrong and... and they had nothing. We apologise and they leave. If they know their rights, and some of them do, they'll shout and scream, threaten all kinds of stuff but they end up none of them doing anything.

The other scenario is if we do suspect someone, but haven't seen anything definite, and the cameras have picked nothing up, what we do is we follow them from the store until we see something, until we can get a conclusive sighting. For instance, they take the item out. Sometimes that as well proves to be a lost cause. They really do have nothing. But most of the time we're proved right.

Pause.

MARION. You were there all the time...

GERRY. I saw you sit on a bench.

MARION. I didn't need to go into any other shops now. I didn't need anything else. I had what I wanted.

GERRY. You just sat there.

MARION. The sun was so warm. I had some time left before I went back.

GERRY. I began to think maybe I'd got it wrong.

MARION. It made me laugh to sit there so near to the store, to the doors I couldn't walk through.

GERRY. You closed your eyes.

MARION. I wanted the sun on my face. I didn't want to go back to work. I wanted to be home and in my room putting the dress on. I closed my eyes. And you stood and watched me.

Pause.

GERRY. It can be a relief to get outside the store sometimes. Into the air. Even if we are still officially working... like, we're following some suspect – even if we are, we're still outside. We're breathing fresh air. The store inside can get so, the air, so stale. And warm. It kind of dulls you sometimes. And we can't rest, none of that. We have to keep on the move – patrolling our floor. He'll be on the radio to us, the security supervisor, if we stand too long somewhere, or if he sees us in the one place too often. So he'll get on the radio and he'll say something. He wants us to be on the move constantly.

And if we want to talk to a colleague, y'know, say hello, how're you doing, on the floor, we have to pretend we want, say, perfume – or on my floor… a… figurine – the porcelain figurines we stock – pretend to be inquiring about one of those while we talk. So that it looks natural. And we have to keep it short. He doesn't want us advertising our presence – that's the point behind it. He doesn't want us giving the game away. He wants us to look as much like customers in the store, shopping, as we can. We have to play them at their own game, he says.

MARION. I let the sun be on my face. I thought of that girl, the changing-room girl. I wondered what it's like to be looked at all the time. To know people are looking at you. She'll know for maybe ten or maybe more years that when people look at her they'll find her pretty and beautiful and they'll want to be near her. She'll have friends who'll meet her anywhere she wants. Men would go and meet her anywhere she said. Men must speak to her all the time. I wondered what that would be like. All the things you could do. You could do anything and people would always be there to help you 'cause they wanted to. I wondered if it would make everything easier for you or would it get on your nerves?

Pause.

GERRY *radios the* SUPERVISOR. *He speaks quietly.*

GERRY. HQ, this is Delta Three… HQ…?

SUPERVISOR. Receiving you, Delta Three. Here I am.

GERRY. I'm still with her, HQ. She's sitting down. We're outside the store. On the pedestrian precinct. She's sitting on one of the benches. The wooden…

SUPERVISOR. I know the benches.

GERRY. But not directly outside.

SUPERVISOR. I sit on those benches from time to time when I have the time. They're wooden.

GERRY. So she's there. She's there.

SUPERVISOR. What is she doing?

GERRY. She's sitting.

SUPERVISOR. That's all?

Her whole life ahead of her. Breathing in the air. All's well in the world. Oh, to be young again.

So. Yeah. Okay. Thank you. Keep me posted.

Pause.

MARION. I only had the afternoon to work now before the week was over and the weekend started. I didn't know where I'd go but I'd end up somewhere. And I had money I could spend. If I went to the pub, the one we always go to, which I hate, if I went in there later on with the dress on, I knew people I know would look at me and say things maybe. And part of me wanted that. I wanted them to speak about me. Instead of what they usually talked about. I wouldn't sit down. I'd just stand by the door, have one drink with my friend and then leave. Put my jacket over my new dress and leave them there. Then head up the town. I didn't know where to but there'd be somewhere. Once I got into town I'd be alright. 'Cause weekends are different. Anything can happen. People look different, they talk different. They dress up. They wear new clothes that they've bought that they never wear any other night. And they get their hair cut or their legs waxed, nails done, eyebrows, just for those two nights. And men and women look at each other and they know each other is there.

GERRY. Sometimes we're following them and we're watching them, we can be with them for fifteen, twenty minutes and we start to wonder who they are – their names. And what they're like. What they do. Not always 'cause you know a lot

of the time the answers are going to be the same – we see so
many of the same kind of person. Other times it's somebody
you just wouldn't think would steal. People with money. And
you're wondering what's made them do it.

Of course we can't think like that too much 'cause that's the
first thing they'll try on with us. They'll try to find a weakness
in us. And out come the sob stories – y'know, the tragic back-
grounds. The dying mother. The junkie boyfriends. The being
treated for depression. Or the period – I'm on my period. It
can get pathetic. 'Cause they'll be in tears or pleading with
you. They'll be desperate; hanging on to you. Please, mate.
Please, mister. Or they… they'll even – they'll offer you
money, some of them. Twenty, thirty, forty quid. They never
have it on them, of course, but they'll send it to you. Or they'll
bring it in to the store tomorrow for us. Or sex. Women
offering us sex to let them go. They'd shag you there and then.
I'll give you a blowjob. These women. Pregnant women. You
can shag me. It's just… 'Cause they'll do anything. Anything.

SUPERVISOR. Delta Three…

GERRY. Roger, HQ?

SUPERVISOR. Mmm. Yeah. I think… I think maybe you
should come back in now, Delta Three.

GERRY. Back in?

SUPERVISOR. Come back in – I think so. Hmm?

What've you got? Nothing. She's a waste of time. I get the
feeling she's a waste of our time.

GERRY. Give me another five minutes, will you, HQ? Come
on. Five minutes.

SUPERVISOR. I'd prefer it if you just came back, Delta Three.
No?

Pause.

GERRY. Should I?

SUPERVISOR. I think you should. There's no shame in it.
There'll be others. There'll always be others.

GERRY. Five minutes isn't long, HQ, is it?

SUPERVISOR. I'm here on my own, Delta Three. I have no one.

Come back, Delta Three. No one will mention it again, I promise. Come back and we'll get you back on third floor and it'll be over.

Delta Three, are you...

GERRY. Wait!

SUPERVISOR. What?

GERRY. She's moving!

SUPERVISOR. Is she?

GERRY. She's going! She's walking.

SUPERVISOR. Are you sure, Delta Three?

GERRY. Of course I'm sure! She's walking. I can see her. She's walking away. I have to go.

SUPERVISOR. Okay, okay... On you go.

Pause.

GERRY. She walked along the pedestrian precinct, along to where it ends and the road starts. She waited for the lights to change to red, then the green man, and crossed over onto Albion Street, and took the first left down Argyle Street. She didn't seem to be in any hurry. I think it was just wandering. I was on the other side, keeping a distance. She kept on down Argyle Street. There was cars parked on both sides and she kept looking in the windows of them, at herself. She fiddled with her hair, raising her hands. I still couldn't see anything. Then she stopped and moved into a doorway. She stood facing it, not going in. Not pressing any of the buzzers there. I knew something was going to happen, and it did. She stood there in the doorway, her back to the street, and unzipped the jacket.

MARION. I wanted to look at it again.

GERRY. She took something green out. Dark green.

MARION. In daylight. The green of it. In natural light.

GERRY. A dress or shirt, something.

MARION. I didn't know if I liked the green.

GERRY. She was staring at it.

MARION. Fifty-four per cent acrylic. Forty-six per cent cotton.

GERRY. I was walking to her.

MARION. I thought – when will I wear it? And where? I'll
never. I knew I'd never wear it. Not even to a wedding or a
special occasion. Dark, is it? – bottle? – bottle green? It'd
hang in my wardrobe and never be worn.

GERRY. Then she folded it. She folded it very carefully. She
was eighteen or nineteen. Not twenty.

MARION. Some black colour moved near me.

GERRY. I was beside her. I got her elbow.

MARION. Something I recognised.

GERRY. I had her elbow. Tight.

MARION (*on street*). Oi…! Get off!

GERRY. I am a…

MARION. What you doing?!

GERRY. I'm a…

MARION. Get away from me!

> I remembered who you were. The man in the store. Who
> looked lost. Buying underwear for his…

> But you weren't. You weren't him. I didn't know who you
> were. You were somebody else.

GERRY. Listen to me. I'm a store detective. Miss…

MARION. No.

GERRY. Miss, please. I have to ask you to accompany me back
to the store, please.

MARION. Miss. Please. Strange language coming out of you.

GERRY. We're told at all times to be polite. To be formal.

MARION. Let go.

GERRY. No.

MARION. Let go.

GERRY. I'm not going to let go.

MARION. I'll scream.

GERRY. Scream. You stole it.

MARION. I never.

GERRY. I saw you.

MARION. You weren't there.

GERRY. I was. I was watching you. You've stolen it. I saw you, darling. You had it in your jacket. I've followed you all the way from the store. Now, you're coming back with me. You hear me? I've asked you. You're coming back with me. 'Cause I don't want to get rough, alright?

MARION. I still had the dress. He hadn't taken it off me. I don't know what I felt. I felt scared. But I was glad it wasn't outside my work. Or inside. I would've died. We stood there. I didn't want to move.

(*On street.*) What'll happen?

GERRY. I'll get you back. We'll speak to you. I don't know. Maybe we'll phone the police.

MARION. No. Don't phone the police. I'm meant to be at work. I start back at two.

GERRY. Should've thought about that before, then, shouldn't you?

MARION. They'll sack me.

GERRY. That's…

MARION. Please…

GERRY. No, no.

MARION. Mister, please...

GERRY. It's not my problem.

MARION. I'm sorry. I'm sorry, I didn't mean it.

GERRY. What d'you think I am?

Pause.

She kind of... I didn't see it coming – just, just... wrenched away from me, away from my hand. I was holding her arm but I didn't have a good enough grip. It was done in a second, like that. I didn't expect it I didn't think she'd try something like that. She started running, the dress still in her hand, out into the road without looking and over to the far side.

It's the last thing they want is to get caught. They risk their lives trying to get away from us. We see it all the time. It's their greatest fear. But, strange, we're always saying that shoplifters, the people who steal from shops, they must always expect to get caught. It must be somewhere in their minds. And they must know that the odds are that one day they will be caught. So in a way they must almost be prepared for it. But no, no, it's as if it never occurred to them that someone was watching them, that someone would want to get the stolen item back from them and so they, I mean they run from us as if they're running for their lives.

Pause.

MARION. I liked your face, Gerry. I remember that.

GERRY. My face?

MARION. I thought you had a nice face.

GERRY. What does that mean?

MARION. When you were there. In the doorway.

GERRY. But what d'you mean – a nice face...?

MARION. Because it was... I thought. Not what...

GERRY. What? Not what? Not what you expected?

MARION. No. It was your eyes. It was your eyes. More than your face. I remember. They looked… I thought they looked kind.

GERRY (*short laugh*). My eyes looked kind…

MARION. Don't laugh.

GERRY. Kind…? I wasn't feeling kind. I was taking you back to call the police. I didn't feel kind. I don't know what you saw. And anyway, the eyes are…

MARION. What?

GERRY. What are they, eyes? Nothing. If you take them out, if you put them in a bowl, they're nothing. Bits of a body.

MARION. I know.

GERRY. So – kind…

MARION. What I mean… What I mean…

GERRY. What do you mean?

MARION. Because I believe the eyes are… are… lit by the person behind them.

We never say that we know anyone until we have looked into their eyes. That is when we feel we have met them. We have an idea about them. But what we do is really look through their eyes. I think.

Have you got children, Gerry?

GERRY. Children?

MARION. Yes.

GERRY. I've got a wife.

Yes, we have children. Two children. Yes. Two.

MARION. And they know what you do?

GERRY. Of course. Of course they do.

MARION. You tell them?

GERRY. Yes.

Pause.

MARION. I pushed the dress back into my jacket. I didn't
know where to go. He was behind me, I could hear him, his
feet hitting the pavement. He'd catch me soon, I knew that. I
kept waiting for him to shout stop, thief! but he never.
People were looking at me anyway, they were standing
watching me run. I hated it. Everyone I passed, turned 'cause
they heard running. I don't know if they knew what was
happening. He still never shouted. I thought he would. I
thought that's what they did. But he just came after me.

GERRY. If they start running, we'll chase them. It's one of the
best parts of the job. The chase. What is it? – the thrill of the
chase…? We are the hunters and they are the hunted. We're
playing with them really.

We can chase them for miles sometimes. I chased a guy for
two hours once. That was five or six years ago. He wouldn't
give up. That was the longest. I don't know if I could do that
now. Another time before that a woman got on a bus and I
ran after it. It was three stops before I caught up with it. I
even had a guy who tried to hail a taxi once, to get away
from me. Imagine that – it's what I'm saying about them –
anything. Imagine flagging down a bloody taxi.

SUPERVISOR (*faintly*). Delta Three…

GERRY. She had it, HQ! She's got something! I saw it!

SUPERVISOR. Delta Three…?

GERRY. I saw it, HQ. I saw it with my own eyes. It was inside
her jacket.

SUPERVISOR. Are you receiving me?

GERRY. I'm chasing her now, HQ.

HQ, I'm chasing her.

SUPERVISOR. I hear you. You're chasing her.

GERRY. I'm chasing her.

SUPERVISOR. Is she running?

GERRY. Yes. I can see her. I'm with her.

SUPERVISOR. Where are you?

GERRY. Eh…

Pause.

SUPERVISOR. The street may have a name, Delta Three. Delta Three, they usually do so that we know where we are.

Pause.

GERRY. I don't know this street. It's not a street I know. It's a side-street.

SUPERVISOR. Which side-street?

GERRY. It's a lane. It's a lane. It has no name.

SUPERVISOR. Where does it lead to, Delta Three? Can you tell me that? Where does it come out?

GERRY. She's heading south.

SUPERVISOR. South.

GERRY. Yes.

SUPERVISOR. If she's heading south then she'll be going across the river, Delta Three. The river, Delta Three, the river. The signals will go. The frequencies will weaken. They won't stand up that far out. I'm going to lose you. You'll end up losing me. You'll be out there on your own.

I want you back, Delta Three.

GERRY. I can get her. I can get her.

SUPERVISOR. It's for the best, believe me.

GERRY. I'm going to get her now. I'm so close. She's fading.

Pause.

SUPERVISOR. You listening to me, Delta Three, are you? Can you hear me? I said I want you back here. I need you here. Delta One and Two are still on lunch. I want you back here. Say something. You're going to get me angry, Delta Three…

His voice gets fainter until it can't be heard. Silence.

MARION. There was a bridge. I saw a bridge and I ran over it.
Because… I don't – it seemed a place he might not follow
me. It seemed a place he might not want to go to. But he
stayed with me. I could still hear his shoes, louder now there
was less traffic. It went over the river, the bridge. The river
was under it, running into the – out to where the sea was. I
don't know which way. Two cars passed me. They drove
near to me. There was more people in them who looked at
me. A man and a woman. I saw the woman pointing, the man
laugh.

Over the bridge, I couldn't choose right or left. I kept on the
pavement. The road went round, and ran beside the river
again. I tried to figure out how old he'd looked. Around forty
maybe. He'd looked quite old. I was surprised.

Across from the river I saw small roads, narrow, going off
the main road. The buildings were all old brick. Dusty brick.
Empty. It was like hundreds of years ago. Streets of buildings where people were once, by the river. Where they
worked probably. There was no cars so I ran over to the road
to one, and down it.

GERRY. We never know where they're running to. We usually
catch them before they get there.

Some of them, I suppose, are running towards their home. If
they have one. Or an area or place they know, somewhere
they know. As long as it's a destination, it's a direction in
which to run. Most of them, we find, run blind, without
thinking. No idea where they're going. They're panicking.
They don't think straight. And what they do, the worst thing,
they always end up running into open space, open areas,
where they're alone, where it's very difficult not to see them.
When what they should be doing is making it difficult for us,
sticking to areas where there's crowds of people, where there
are people, where there's buildings or, or… which will
obscure our view of them. Instead, they stay on their own
and make it simple for us.

(*On street he shouts.*) That's alright, love! You keep going!

MARION. He shouted something at me.

Didn't you?

GERRY. Yes.

MARION. What was it?

GERRY. We always do it

MARION. I heard love. You called me love.

GERRY (*running*). That's alright, love. You keep going! I've got all day! I've got all the time in the world!

MARION. I've got all the time in the world.

GERRY. It's something we always do.

MARION. Why?

GERRY. I don't know – to…

MARION. It scared me.

GERRY. Well, to scare you. Then it worked. It's meant to scare you. It's meant to unnerve you. I am right here. I won't go away.

MARION. I didn't understand you.

GERRY. It's plain English. We all shout it.

I saw her react when I shouted. They always do. It makes them nervous. They don't know what to make of it. That kind of personal touch. That… that… familiarity. As if the, yes the two of us are bound together. We call the women love or darling or sweetheart. If they're women. The men are just mate. Or wanker. Depends.

She'd gone, after the bridge, gone right, turned right. Along the roadway by the river. She was flagging. I could see it in her run. Adelphi Street, it was. Then over it, into, it was Ashfield Street.

Where were you going?

MARION. I don't know.

GERRY. You were just running?

MARION. I couldn't think. You were catching me up.

GERRY. I know.

MARION. I knew you were. I was tired. I was sweating. My
jacket was too warm.

Pause.

At the end was a wall. Blocking the street off. They'd built a
wall right across the street, I don't know why. I couldn't go
anywhere now. I turned round. He'd seen it. He'd seen the
wall. He knew about it. He was just walking towards me. I
could see his chest rising, taking in air. The sun was in my
eyes, scorching my face. I couldn't breathe.

GERRY. These streets were used when the river was busy. Ten,
twenty years ago. And before that. The buildings had arch-
ways bricked over. The doors were padlocked and windows
smashed. They would unload cargo from ships at the river-
side and store it in these buildings before it went on to other
places. No one ever lived here. Only worked. She sat with
her back against the wall. The bricks in it were newer than
the rest of the street. She put her head on her arms. She
waited for me to come to her. That was it.

*Both panting heavily. When they speak at first the words are
gasped. MARION recovers her breath some time before
GERRY.*

Just you stay there... Hear me?

She nodded. Her face was red.

MARION. I felt sick. I hadn't run so far in years. Jesus... I
couldn't move. My legs hurt. I wanted to be sick. The sun
was in my eyes.

GERRY. I'm warning you...

MARION. I heard you...

GERRY. Don't try anything...

MARION. He was standing ahead of me. He was sweating, I
could see it. He was bent over a bit, holding his side, gulping
air down.

GERRY. When they're finally caught, we've cornered them somewhere or they're exhausted and can't go a step further – they always look the same. They look at you and they are so... so... pitiful. So many of them are so young. This person you were chasing, who was running because they thought they had a chance has now become like a... a wounded animal. Who wants put out its misery. It's the end and they're defenceless. And there's part of you that feels pity. You can't help it. Because... because there is nothing left for them. And I... I mean, we... we are seeing people in one of the worst states you can see them. Hope abandoned. Not caring now what happens to them. It's not something you want to see too much.

Christ, you nearly killed me... You don't give up, do you? Right, c'mon you, on your feet.

MARION. Give me a minute.

GERRY (*coughs loudly*). Jesus...

MARION. Can you not just take it?

GERRY. She held the dress out.

Short laugh.

I don't believe you!

MARION. Please, mister...

GERRY. Doesn't work like that, sorry. No.

MARION. Please...

GERRY. Better save your breath for walking back.

MARION. I'll give you money.

GERRY. You got money on you?

MARION. Yeah.

GERRY. Should've bought that then, shouldn't you? That's what money's for.

MARION. How much do you want?

GERRY. I don't want anything.

MARION. I've got more in my bank. I can get it out. You can
have it.

GERRY. You can say anything you want to me, love. It doesn't
matter. Nothing matters. It's too late. All that happens is I
take you back with me. That's all. So c'mon. On your feet.

MARION. I'm going to be sick.

GERRY. Be sick. Be sick. Then you get up.

Nothing coming?

MARION. What's your name?

GERRY. No, no.

MARION. You got any children?

GERRY. I won't tell you again. Stand up.

MARION. I can't. My legs have gone. I can't walk.

GERRY. I'll just pull you up. Believe me. I'll pull you up.

MARION. Don't you touch me! Stay away from me!

He grabs her, hauls her up.

Awwhhh…

GERRY. Legs are fine, see.

MARION. You're a dirty bastard!

GERRY. I know, I know.

MARION. You're hurting me!

GERRY. You ready now?

MARION. You don't have to hold me so tight.

GERRY. You stay beside me. You walk beside me. I'm not
going to let you go. You do nothing, you try nothing – you
hear? Now give me that.

MARION. I don't even want it.

I threw the dress on the ground.

GERRY. What d'you do that for? Eh? What's that for? Pick it up.

MARION. No. Pick it up. I'm not going to. Pick it up.

SUPERVISOR*'s voice, faint. Radio crackling with static.*

SUPERVISOR. Delta Three…?

GERRY. Pick it up.

SUPERVISOR. Delta… (*Static.*) You there…?

MARION. Is that your name – Delta Three?

GERRY. Shut up.

MARION. You not going to answer him? Is that your boss? You should…

GERRY. Shut up. Be quiet. Pick it…

SUPERVISOR. Delta Three…

GERRY. Don't say a word. Stand there.

HQ, this is Delta Three… HQ…

SUPERVISOR. Delta Three…?

GERRY. What is it, HQ?

SUPERVISOR. Delta Three… What's… (*Static.*)

GERRY. HQ, I have the girl.

SUPERVISOR. Repeat, Delta Three…

GERRY. I have… the girl…

SUPERVISOR. You have her?

GERRY. Roger.

SUPERVISOR. With you?

GERRY. Right here with me, HQ. I'm bringing her back.

SUPERVISOR. Great news, Delta Three… (*Static.*) Great, great news. I am a happy man… Get her back here as fast… (*Static. Cuts off.*)

GERRY. Now.

MARION. What?

GERRY. Are you going to pick it up?

MARION. What for?

SUPERVISOR. Delta Three…?

GERRY. Such a stupid thing. Look at it. All this way for that. Look at it. Lying on the ground. What is it now? Why didn't you think?

MARION. I don't care. I don't need it now, do I?

GERRY. I'm going to pick it up. I'm not letting you go. I'm going to bend down…

MARION. Agh… That hurts.

GERRY. I wanted it to hurt.

It was a kind of shiny fabric, I don't know what. There was nothing to it. It was so small.

Right. We're off. On our travels.

They start walking. Sound of the occasional car.

MARION. You'll get the police, will you?

GERRY. Mm?

MARION. You'll get the police?

GERRY. Mm-hmm.

MARION *sighs. They walk. Pause.*

This your first time?

MARION. Yes. It is.

GERRY. Would say that, though, wouldn't you?

MARION. I've never done this before in my life.

GERRY. You'll get a caution probably then.

MARION. What's that mean?

GERRY. A ticking off. They'll say don't you do it again.

MARION. I'm never going through this again.

D'you like it? You're looking at it. D'you like it?

GERRY. Is this what they wear now?

MARION. You were looking at the dress. Why?

GERRY. It was dark green. Bottle, is it? Bottle green?

MARION. Nice, isn't it?

GERRY. It had these thin, thin shoulder straps. So thin they looked like shoelaces.

How much were they wanting for this?

MARION. Fifty.

GERRY. For this?

MARION. Course. You have to pay that to look good. It's for the weekend. It's a Saturday-night dress.

GERRY. It was so small. And short. Left nothing to the imagination. How old are you?

MARION. What for?

GERRY. Just asking.

MARION. Nineteen.

GERRY. D'you work?

MARION. Uh-huh.

GERRY. Where?

MARION. Somewhere.

A hospital. I'm a heart surgeon. I should be getting back.

GERRY. Glad you can still make jokes.

MARION. Lost my job anyway now.

GERRY. What…?

MARION (*simultaneous with* GERRY*'s* '*What…?*'). What age…?

GERRY. What?

MARION. What age are you? You're old.

GERRY. Am I?

MARION. I think so.

GERRY. Depends how you see it, doesn't it? 'Cause my father thinks I'm young.

MARION. You looked across the river. At where we'd come from. Where we were going. You were still holding the dress.

D'you like young girls, do you?

GERRY. Eh?

MARION. Is nineteen young enough?

GERRY. Shut up.

MARION. 'Cause I could put the...

GERRY. I said shut up.

MARION. Put the dress on for you. We could find somewhere quiet. You could...

GERRY. Walk.

MARION. Watch me undress...

GERRY. No.

MARION. I'll put it on.

GERRY. Walk, I said.

MARION. No? You don't want that? 'Cause you can touch me.

GERRY. Shut your mouth, will you!

Pause.

MARION. Sorry. I thought that's what you wanted.

GERRY. I've had enough of you.

MARION. Do you want to kiss me?

GERRY. No. No, I don't want to kiss you.

MARION. Can I kiss you?

GERRY. No, you can't.

MARION. Just a wee one?

GERRY. Don't do this.

MARION. C'mon...

GERRY. Listen to yourself.

MARION. You should get a...

GERRY. Can you hear yourself?

MARION. A reward. For catching me.

She leans towards him.

GERRY. Don't...

He recoils.

MARION. Just a peck.

GERRY. No...

She spits loudly in his face.

Awh...

She pulls away from him. Starts running again.

You little bitch! Shit!

Begins running again.

She got away from me. She spat at me. They'll stop at nothing. I've been spat at, scratched, kicked, punched, head-butted. Everything. I've been called every name under the sun. They've threatened me. They've promised to kill me. They've said they'll come and kill my wife and children. They're animals, most of them. Wild animals.

MARION. D'you know why? I knew.

GERRY. Knew what? You knew what?

MARION. I knew what you were going to do.

GERRY. What?

MARION. I saw it. In your eyes.

GERRY. I told you...

MARION. Because you were holding the dress.

GERRY. Yes.

MARION. And you wanted to let me go. Weren't you? You were going to take your hand away and let me go. I saw it in your eyes. I could see it in your face.

GERRY. You saw nothing in my face.

MARION. That's what you were about to say.

GERRY. There was nothing in my eyes.

MARION. Because...

GERRY. No. My eyes...? I told you. What do you...

MARION. Looking at the dress...

GERRY. ...think I am?

MARION. The dress I stole with the thin, thin shoulder straps like shoelaces. The fifty-quid dress and how little there was of it. I know because I saw.

It was the desperation. My desperation. Wanting that dress. Because of what it promised. The dress I'd never wear. Where would I wear a dress like that? That was it, Gerry, wasn't it? That's what happened. I saw it in your face. In your eyes. The wounded animal put out of its misery.

GERRY. You little bitch!

Them both running, both breathing. GERRY*'s heavier.*

MARION. That was it, Gerry, wasn't it?

GERRY. No.

MARION. Of course it was.

GERRY. I had the dress.

MARION. I know.

GERRY. So why did I chase you?

MARION. Because… Why? What else could you do, Gerry? What else could you do? You had no choice.

GERRY. Then I tripped. I fell. I hit the pavement.

He falls heavily, hitting concrete.

Uh… I put my hands out to break the fall but my knees hit first. I seemed to slide on the concrete. I felt gravel on my face and palms, biting into them.

(*Groans.*) Aww…

She stopped. I heard her stop.

MARION. You were still holding the dress.

You alright? Mister? You alright?

She walks closer to him.

Mister?

GERRY. You were standing above me.

MARION. Your eyes were closed.

GERRY. I could feel the sun on my face. Burning the sweat. My face was stinging.

MARION. Mister…

GERRY. I tried to grab her ankle. I thought: I'll grab onto her ankle. I'll hold onto her ankle. I put my hand out but it went so slow. She would've seen it. It moved so slowly in the heat. She stepped back. She saw my hand come out.

The dress was pulled out of my hand. I felt the material sliding under my hand.

I had to get up. I had to get on my feet. She was walking away from me.

SUPERVISOR. Delta Three... This is HQ. Delta Three, Delta One and Two are back from their lunch. They're with me now. They're standing here with me now, wondering where you are. We're all waiting to hear from you.

MARION. He was on his feet again. Unsteady.

GERRY. I shouted at you.

MARION. I heard you.

GERRY. Stupid.

MARION. Come back.

GERRY. Come back, you!

Why did I shout that? She started running again.

GERRY*'s laboured breathing.*

SUPERVISOR. Delta Three...? Is that you I can hear? Panting like an old dog? Is that you wheezing like an old woman. I shouldn't have let you go, should I? I shouldn't have let you out the door. I should've kept you on the third floor where you belong.

GERRY. The last thing she did, she turned and shouted at me. She shouted something back at me.

MARION. It made me laugh.

GERRY. You called me love.

MARION *laughs.*

MARION. Just like you. I'm the same as you, Gerry, now. I'm the same as you.

GERRY. What d'you mean?

MARION. Do you see what you've done...? Gerry? Do you see what you've done?

GERRY. What do you mean?

MARION. Where do I go now? I've no one left. I've no home. I've no family. I've nothing. I'm left with nothing. I've nowhere to run to.

GERRY. And she ran. She ran across the road. And shouted.

MARION. C'mon, love! Keep up! I've got all day! I've got all the time in the world!

GERRY. No…!

Sound of a car braking. Skidding. It hits MARION.

Aw Jesus… Aw Jesus…

He runs towards her. Sound of a car door opening. GERRY *shouts at the driver.*

Get an ambulance! Quick! Get an ambulance!

The driver runs off.

Adelphi Street! This is Adelphi Street! Near the bridge!

He kneels down where MARION *is lying.*

Aw Jesus…

MARION (*muffled*). Where am I?

GERRY. It's alright. I've got you. It's alright.

MARION. Where…

GERRY. It's okay. You're okay. You're okay, darling.

SUPERVISOR. Delta Three… come in, please…

GERRY *pulls the radio off, throws it as far as he can. Sound of it bouncing on concrete.*

MARION. What is it?

GERRY. You fell. You fell down. You're okay. You're okay. What's your name? Darling, what's your name? Tell me your name?

My name's Gerry. I'm Gerry. I've got you. You're okay. I'm holding on to you. You'll be alright.

She was wearing a blue jacket. And she was nineteen, twenty, twenty-one. About that. Twenty, twenty-one. Blue jacket and white jeans. And white trainers. Her hair was up. She'd tied it up like a lot of them… Tied up. Tied back.

There was blood in her hair. Blood was coming out of her head somewhere. It was in her mouth. Her face was white. She was shivering. She couldn't speak. I held her. I stayed beside her. I wiped the blood away from her eyes.

SUPERVISOR*'s voice coming from the distant radio.*

SUPERVISOR. We don't want you back here without her, Delta Three. We don't want you coming back with nothing to show for yourself. If you haven't got her then don't bother coming back. Don't show up here at all. Just go home. Go home and have a sit down. Have a think. We'll see you back here tomorrow morning. We can sit down all of us and have a talk. You, me and Delta One and Two. We'll all sit down and have a talk. HQ, over and out, Delta Three. HQ, over and out.

The End.

HARM

Douglas Maxwell

Douglas Maxwell was born in 1974 in Girvan, a small town on the Ayrshire coast of Scotland. He is the author of many plays including *Decky Does a Bronco*, *Our Bad Magnet*, *Variety*, *If Destroyed True*, *Backpacker Blues*, *Melody*, *The Ballad of James II* and *Harm*. His work for young people includes *Helmet*, *Beyond* (with Nicola McCartney), *Mancub* and *The Mother Ship* (Brian Way Award for Best Play for a Younger Audience, 2009).

2010 saw three of his plays tour Scotland and abroad: *Promises Promises* for Random Accomplice; *The Miracle Man* for the National Theatre of Scotland; and a musical for Cumbernauld Theatre called *The Bookie*. His iconic play *Decky Does a Bronco* was also remounted for a major tour by Grid Iron. The *Scotsman* called it 'one of the finest plays to emerge from a Scottish working-class story in the last ten years'.

Future productions include his version of Wedekind's *Spring Awakening* for Grid Iron and the Traverse Theatre; a new work for young performers called *Too Fast* for the Royal National Theatre's New Connections; a comedy called *Small Town* co-written with Johnny McKnight and DC Jackson; and a television adaptation of his play *Mancub* for BBC Scotland.

Douglas Maxwell currently lives in Glasgow with his wife, Caroline Newall and his daughter Ellis.

Harm was commissioned by Sweetscar as part of the Sure Shots season, and first performed at the Tron Theatre, Glasgow, on 12 September 2006, with the following cast:

FATHER   Stewart Porter
SON   Mark Wood

Director   Adrian Osmond
Designer   Kirsty Mackay
Lighting Designer   Malcolm Rogan
Producer   Purni Morell

Characters

FATHER

SON

Note

In 2006, St George's Hospital in Staffordshire began a pilot project where young people who self-harm can do so in a 'clean, supervised environment'.

Underneath the hopeful posters and booklets,

Behind the covered couch,

Below the happy curtains and the 'it'll do for now' table

Is a hospital room.

A clean, supervised environment

Where once upon a time

People died.

You can't hide that.

Here's a FATHER. *Here's a* SON.

A nurse has just left the room

And this vacuum is what they've both been dreading.

The FATHER *remembers (just in time) that he's got a booklet in his hand.*

He reads it.

FATHER. 'A clean, supervised environment.'

We're probably being supervised now, I should think. That's probably a camera. Do you think? Or was she the supervision? Maybe she sits in. Do you think she sits in?

No. It'll be cameras. Everything's cameras. Cameras everywhere. It's like that film you used to love, isn't it? What's it called again? That film. You used to have the poster on your door, mind? What's it called? Help me out, mate, what's that film called?

It'll come back to me.

Hey, if it is her that's supervising she's not doing a very good job, eh? Day one of Supervising School: 'Stay in the room.' Did you see that graffiti in the lift? 'This lift can hold up to fifteen people' and someone's written underneath 'Or three nurses'. Must've been talking about her, eh?

Nah. Shouldn't ridicule the fat.

Don't know why, though, they bring it on themselves, don't they? Not like they're born eating a pie roll. They *decided* to buy that pie roll and they *decided* to eat it. It's just a stupid, greedy, selfish...

Habit.

Or maybe not, I don't know. Genetics.

God, that was a faff getting out here, though, eh? Two buses.

I should have a car again soon.

Mind you, it'll be your mother that brings you next time. If there is a next time. But today's my day and that's that.

Still. Has to be done.

Much better doing it here in a clean, supervised environment than at home. Isn't it? More official.

Everything's sterilised. You've got your bandages and that all laid out. Razors. Lighters. Lighters?

Yup. Says here. 'Lighters.'

Oh aye, says that after a while they get you onto alternatives. That's good, isn't it? 'Ice cubes on the skin, flicking the arm with elastic bands, behavioural therapy sessions.' God I'd rather flick my arm with an elastic band than see another bloody therapist any day. Now, if they let you flick a therapist with an elastic band it'd be worth the trip, eh?

No, it's good.

This is good.

That's bugging me now. That film you wouldn't shut up about, what is it again? C'mon. Sunglasses were involved. What was it called?

I got you the DVD one of my Sundays, remember? When we couldn't get into the pool. You were delighted. I remember it. Very clearly.

It's not important.

Oh hey, I got that album. The one you were playing last time
you were over. Murder of Crows. Strong stuff. Pretty intense.
But good. Powerful. That last track. Very good. Yeah, I think
I'll definitely be checking them out again. Excellent.
Reminded me a bit of a band I used to listen to. You won't
have heard of them. The Clash? No. Before your time. I had
all the gear. Good band. Maybe I'll look you out one of their
tapes. I think it's... I think I've still a couple. Somewhere.

I suppose as well, coming here, they weed out the ones that
are just pretending. Know what I mean? The ones that are
just copying some idiot from TV or from some band or
something. The kiddy-on ones would never come all the way
out here. Two buses. No way.

I mean, if it's just pretend, that's just...

Final-straw stuff.

My old man died in this hospital. You know that? Yeah.
Grandpa Jim. Somewhere here. I don't think it was this room.
Could've been, I suppose. They've done it all up since.

I was late. I missed it. Mind you, I was right in the middle of
all that... stuff. I wouldn't've been much good to anyone.
You were there, though. You were a wee baby.

Mum grabbed you right out of my arms. She thought I was
going to drop you. But I wouldn't've. I've never done that.
No way. It's not happening.

But she grabs you and takes you over to the body and starts
rubbing your wee baby hands all over his eyes. I thought,
'Christ, don't tell me she's lost it as well.' But apparently it
means you'll only ever have good thoughts of him. The dead
person. You didn't cry.

I couldn't do it.

I couldn't even touch him.

Maybe I should've.

But you did. And no tears. So.

I remember thinking, 'I hope this means Jamie's going to be brave like his grandpa.'

And you're not a crier. Are you? Even to this day. No tears.

No anything.

Oh. Is it The Something Revolution? That film? It is. Something Something Revolution, or something.

No. No memory. I must be lying again. Another fantasy that you can all deny.

There was never a film. There was never a poster. You were never delighted.

Sake.

God knows what he would've said to all of this.

Something definite. He was a definite man. Even when he was shouting it was a clear order: 'Do not do that do this!'

Maybe it was the boxing. Make your decision and bam!

I used to beg him to teach me. But nah. It belonged to him. When he died we found a box of trophies in the hut. Know that? He had them hidden. I've got them in the flat now. Next time you're round.

I just wanted to see him do it. Just once. I remember I made up this story that I was getting bullied. Told him I was terrified. Just to... I don't know. But nah. He just said, 'Tell your teacher.' Wouldn't let me... wouldn't let me in.

I think that's good, though. That's right. That's what made him strong.

A good father. A good man.

That's where I've...

I think I'm...

Cos, sometimes I think, like, that night when you and your sister came in and I was all... you know... crying and... all that stuff, that maybe, that was the start of it.

Was it?

Jamie?

Was that night the start of it? When you saw me like that?

Well, I'm going to be strong from now on in. I promise. Hear me? I promise. I can feel it. Clean slate.

Okay, mate? Both of us.

We'll be fine.

This is… this'll be a funny story in a few years. Okay?

Yeah. Good man.

He used to pull out his eyelashes. Grandpa Jim. He didn't know I knew, but I did. I could see him from my window. Sitting on the garden step, pulling out his eyelashes, listening to Gaelic songs on the radio. He'd hold them in his hand and just look at them, like he was amazed at what he'd done. Then he'd throw them in the grass. I'd go down there, after he was in his bed and try to find them. But it was just impossible.

He'd hate folk knowing about that.

Hey, I wonder if that counts? I wonder if he was your age now, if he'd have to sit in this room and pull out his eyelashes while that big fat nurse supervises?

Eh?

Ach well.

I'll… em… I'll be outside, I suppose.

I don't think we need to wait for her to come back. It's probably cameras.

Just…

Well.

Make sure you…

Jamie?

Don't do it.

Don't do it.

Just don't do it, Jamie.

Please.

Please, son.

Let's just go away from here. Let's just go home and see Mum and… and… *hold* each other or something.

For God's sake.

Why can't we just hold each other?

For God's sake!

For God's sake.

Why can't we just… do something like that?

For…

DON'T YOU DARE DO IT JAMIE WILSON DO YOU UNDERSTAND ME?

I AM YOUR FATHER AND I'M TELLING YOU FOR THE LAST TIME!

I AM ORDERING YOU NOT TO DO IT.

YOU ARE FORBIDDEN.

Please. Please. Please. Please.

The FATHER *makes a quick move to the door.*

SON. Dad.

You don't need to go.

You can stay.

If you want to.

The FATHER *folds to the ground.*

The SON *goes to him.*

They nearly hold each other.

FATHER. I'm doing alright.

SON. I know you are.

FATHER. I'm doing good.

SON. I know you are.

The SON *leaves his* FATHER *and starts what he came here to do.*

He sets up the blades the way he always does

And takes off his shirt.

A fucking howl from the FATHER

When he sees his baby's body

Ripped, scarred, bloody,

Bruised, from a life in the ring.

FATHER. I did that to you.

SON. No you didn't.

The SON *puts the blade to his chest*

And slashes a clear, bright cut.

The FATHER *feels the blade slash open his ribcage.*

Another.

The FATHER *feels this one cut open his heart.*

Another

Another

Another

The End.

THE BASEMENT FLAT

Rona Munro

Rona Munro has written extensively for stage, radio, film and television including the award-winning plays *Iron*, *Bold Girls*, and *The Maiden Stone*. Other recent credits include *The Last Witch* (Edinburgh International Festival); *Long Time Dead* (Paines Plough); *The Indian Boy* (Royal Shakespeare Company); *Mary Barton* (Royal Exchange Theatre) and *Watership Down* (Lyric Hammersmith). Her work for film and television includes the Ken Loach film, *Ladybird, Ladybird*, *Aimee and Jaguar*, and the BBC television dramas *Rehab* and *Bumping the Odds* (nominated for the BAFTA for best single drama, 1998). She has also written many other single plays for radio and television and contributed to series including *Casualty* and *Dr Who*. Current projects include the play *Little Eagles* (Royal Shakespeare Company, 2011) and the film *Oranges and Sunshine*, starring Emily Watson and Hugo Weaving.

The Basement Flat was first performed at the Traverse Theatre, Edinburgh, on 13 August 2009, with the following cast:

FIONA	Cora Bissett
STEPHEN	Matthew Pidgeon
Director	Roxana Silbert

Characters

FIONA

STEPHEN

FIONA *and* STEPHEN *are sitting in silence, piles of mail and paperwork around them.*

There are the sounds of heavy footsteps overhead. FIONA *looks up.*

FIONA. He can't sleep either.

STEPHEN *says nothing. He pulls some letters towards him, gets busy with a laptop calculator.*

Thing is… I do feel sorry for him… in a way.

STEPHEN *is rapidly entering figures.*

Don't you?

STEPHEN *is reading the result of his calculations. He groans in dismay.*

Just a little bit?

STEPHEN. What?

FIONA. Feel sorry for him?

STEPHEN (*quiet, almost to himself*). No, I fucking don't.

He starts entering figures again.

FIONA. He wanted this so much. Sooooo much.

Pause.

I knew that as soon as he moved in, as soon as I saw those window boxes. Remember the little terracotta window boxes he had…? From the nice garden shop, you know, with the olive trees and the galvanised-steel planters… and the Cath Kidston aprons…

I wanted a Cath Kidston apron for my birthday.

And a matching shoulder bag.

And the oven-glove set... It would be so decorative. You could hang it on a hook and it would be kitchen decoration, really...

STEPHEN. Yeah well, I'm sorry...

FIONA. No, no... the soap was fine. Lovely. Almost as good as Molton Brown... Well, it had real floral scent in it... I think... nice liquid soap. That's a little bit of luxury...

Just simple things. That's all you need, isn't it? A bit of pampering... every time you wash your hands.

Pause.

You can't see the window boxes for dead ivy. All his ivy's dead.

Did you hear me?

STEPHEN. What?!

FIONA. The ivy. In his lovely terracotta window boxes. It's all dead.

STEPHEN. I think we'll have to rent out the second bedroom.

FIONA. What?

STEPHEN. I don't see an alternative, not if we're going to get through this.

FIONA. Susan's bedroom?!

STEPHEN. She's not using it, Fiona.

FIONA. She is! All her stuff is there!

STEPHEN. She's gone.

FIONA. She hasn't gone! She's only out there!

FIONA *is pointing at the dark garden outside.*

STEPHEN. Yes. She's out there now. She's gone.

FIONA. Not far! And she comes back!

STEPHEN. When did you last see her?

FIONA. Only a few days ago! Last week!

STEPHEN. Really?

FIONA. I did!

He doesn't believe her.

I did!!

STEPHEN. Did she say anything?

FIONA. She looked lovely. Fit and healthy...

STEPHEN. What did she say to you?

FIONA. She was in a hurry. She couldn't stop.

STEPHEN. You didn't see her.

FIONA. I saw her! She was here! She was running across the back of the lawn...

STEPHEN. It's not a lawn, is it? It's a jungle. That bloody lawn broke my strimmer.

FIONA. Can't we afford to get it done? Just the bit near the house?

STEPHEN. No.

I'll get a scythe. Do it the old-fashioned way. Sweat and dirt. Hack the whole thing down... Plant potatoes.

A vegetable garden. That's the way forward. Self-sufficiency.

FIONA. It all comes down to slugs and snails.

STEPHEN. Does it?

FIONA. My granddad had an allotment. It was a war against slugs. Twenty-four seven. I haven't got the energy, Stephen. I don't.

STEPHEN. People used to do it.

FIONA. People were used to slugs back then.

STEPHEN. Well, I'm going to hack down that fucking fox run.

FIONA. Don't!

Please.

Don't.

STEPHEN. I think we should move her stuff into boxes and clear out that room.

FIONA. At least wait till I've asked her. Let me talk to her first.

STEPHEN. Are you sure she still talks?

Footsteps overhead.

He was asking about her.

FIONA. What do you mean?

STEPHEN. She's been damaging things.

FIONA. What things?

STEPHEN. Around the house.

FIONA. What?

STEPHEN. Structural damage. To the house.

FIONA. He never said.

STEPHEN. He said it to me.

FIONA. I can't see any damage.

STEPHEN. The bricks. The mortar.

FIONA. Well, how could she do that?

STEPHEN. He saw her.

FIONA. Then he should have talked to her. Told her to come home!

STEPHEN. The thing is… It is his house.

FIONA. This bit is still ours!

STEPHEN. Yes, but… In terms of how we manage things… It is his house now.

FIONA. We should never have signed those papers.

STEPHEN. What choice did we have?

Pause.

I thought he'd know how to manage things.

FIONA. He can't even manage a window box!

Pause.

Is that more damp?

STEPHEN. Where?

FIONA. On the wall there...

He looks.

STEPHEN (*resigned*). Yes.

FIONA. I thought he was going to sort out the damp.

Looks like a big fish swimming down the wall... A whale...

STEPHEN. He wants us to pay for a security fence.

FIONA. What for?

STEPHEN. To stop her doing any more damage.

FIONA. She's our daughter!

STEPHEN. That's his point.

That's why he wants us to pay.

FIONA *says nothing, shocked and angry.*

Don't feel so sorry for him now, do you?

FIONA. That's too much. We've got to take a stand now. I'm going to talk to him. I'm going to have words with him.

STEPHEN. Now?!

FIONA. Yes!

Hesitates.

No...

Maybe not now... In the morning...

STEPHEN. Well... you have to ask yourself... what good would it do? He'll just do what he wants anyway, won't he?

FIONA. He can't make us pay for a security fence, Stephen.

STEPHEN. He'll bill us.

Won't he?

FIONA. And we'll refuse to pay!

STEPHEN. And then what? It's his house, Fiona.

FIONA. We won't let him build the thing, Stephen. I'm not going to stand by and let that man keep our daughter from her own bed with barbed wire and electricity! I won't!

STEPHEN. Well, what are you going to do?

FIONA. I'll tell him!

STEPHEN. And when he builds it anyway? And bills us? What are you going to do?

FIONA. I won't have it! I won't!

STEPHEN. What are you going to do?

Pause.

FIONA. It's not right! It's not fair!

STEPHEN. I know. But what can you do?

FIONA. She's our daughter! It's our house too!

STEPHEN. We signed it away, Fiona.

FIONA (*quiet*). We didn't…

STEPHEN. Excuse me?

FIONA. Nothing.

STEPHEN. No, go on, say it.

FIONA. We didn't sign it away.

STEPHEN. Go on.

FIONA. You know what I'm saying.

STEPHEN. I'd like to hear you say it… again.

FIONA. You didn't stop him. That's all. You could have gone down to the lawyer's. You could have said those were only draft documents. You could have got there well before the deadline…

STEPHEN. And where were you?

FIONA. You could have stopped him owning the rights to the whole house…

STEPHEN. And where were you when I rang and said I was held up with Peter from work?

FIONA. In a bar, you were held up in a bloody wine bar…

STEPHEN. Where were you?

FIONA. You know where I was!

STEPHEN. At the hairdresser's!

FIONA. She'd put my foils in! What did you want me to do!?

STEPHEN. Get down the lawyer's and hold on to our bricks and mortar!

FIONA. You said you were going to do it!

STEPHEN. I was working!

FIONA. In a wine bar?

STEPHEN. Yes! Working!

So, how expensive were your highlights in the end, Fiona?

Pause.

FIONA. You said it didn't matter. You said…

STEPHEN. I know what I said.

Pause.

FIONA (*mimicking his tone*). 'No biggy.'

STEPHEN. I know!

Pause.

We both thought it would be fine. We both thought it was better. Financially…

FIONA. We were better off.

STEPHEN. My God, it was a dream come true! We're still better off than a lot of people. We have to remember that. We're safe at least.

Pause.

FIONA. I thought we could have a terrace. With an olive tree.

STEPHEN. It's too cold for olive trees.

FIONA. It's not. Open the window. It's hot, dark, jungle.

Pause.

It's all the houses on the road, in the whole area... the hedges are just getting...

STEPHEN. There's no pavement left...

FIONA. But it's more than that! There's things... rustling in there...

STEPHEN. It's rats. You seen the size of the rats since they stopped collecting the rubbish?

FIONA. I think it's kids.

STEPHEN. Well, of course it's the kids too. We know that.

FIONA. Why would anyone want to be living in a hedge!? They should be in school!

STEPHEN. Some of them are...

FIONA (*not hearing him*). They should be sitting their exams not running around with wild street kids from God knows where...

Beat.

She was chasing the foxes... Her hair... Oh I wanted to comb out her hair... It's the same colour as the foxes... all of them shining copper in the sun... running...

STEPHEN. He says she's been biting the stones...

FIONA. Last thing she said to me... 'All you care about is this house. Bricks and mortar. I hope they crumble and bury you alive.'

STEPHEN. Scratching them, she's been scratching out the mortar.

FIONA. That's ridiculous! How could she scratch out...?

STEPHEN (*cutting in*). He says she's grown claws.

FIONA (*uncertain*). Well that's just ridiculous. He's cracking up.

Footsteps overhead.

I still don't want to think he's a bad man. He's just weak.

STEPHEN. I thought he knew what he was doing.

FIONA. We both did.

STEPHEN. Look at the cracks in the wall there.

FIONA. We can't leave. We can't just leave. This house is all we've got.

Crumbling bricks and mortar.

STEPHEN. I mean that's basic! Basic maintenance. You can't leave cracks untended. Anything could get in, rain, ice... anything.

FIONA. When he said he wanted to take on the house I was relieved.

STEPHEN. Well, it was too much for us!

FIONA. I trusted him. He has such a trustworthy face. Big dogged... dog face. A chin you can put your faith in...

STEPHEN. Really... really what we are now is tenants, life tenants in a house that should still be ours.

FIONA. We own this!

STEPHEN. Under his rules! Under his documents. His say-so!

FIONA. It's ours! We paid for it.

STEPHEN. We can't afford it.

FIONA. I thought he'd love it. He wanted it so much. I thought he'd bring it back to its glory days... shining windows... tended hedges... safe and warm and dry...

I'm being punished. We're being punished because we wanted to sit on our patio under an olive tree and drink Sunday coffee and never worry about cleaning out the gutters.

STEPHEN. We're still better off than a lot of people. We're…
safe. Aren't we?

FIONA. I don't know. If you say so.

Pause.

STEPHEN. He's got a gun.

FIONA. What?!

STEPHEN. Until a fence goes up. He showed me. He's got a
gun.

FIONA. He can't do that!

STEPHEN. He can do whatever he likes. He's making the rules,
isn't he?

Pause.

FIONA. Just a cup of coffee, on the patio…

STEPHEN. There's weeds on the patio.

FIONA. I thought global warming would give us Tuscan sun.
It's just this terrible hot, dirty rain…

STEPHEN. The gutters are choked with leaves. There's ivy
coming down the chimneys…

FIONA. The rats are probably here already, aren't they? In the
pipes.

STEPHEN. He can't even keep out the weather! He's not going
to keep out the rain with a bloody gun, is he?

An animal howl outside.

FIONA. Oh!

Another howl.

Oh Stephen, did you hear that?

STEPHEN. Of course I fucking heard it!

They listen. Nothing.

FIONA. Was it…? Do you think it was her?

STEPHEN. Oh God, I hope not. I really hope not.

FIONA (*starting to cry*). I want her to come home! I just want her where I can see her!

STEPHEN. Fiona...

FIONA. I just want to touch her!

STEPHEN. I know.

It could have been any of them. That's the truth. We can't know...

FIONA. Open the door!

STEPHEN. We don't know it's her.

FIONA. Please, Stephen.

STEPHEN. It's dark. We can't risk it. We don't know what's out there any more.

FIONA. Open the window! Let me call her!

STEPHEN. They won't budge. It's the damp, the creepers growing over the wood...

FIONA. I have to believe she might come home.

STEPHEN. She will! One day when she's...

FIONA. She doesn't need us!

She doesn't need to live in a house. She's no reason... to come back.

Pause.

STEPHEN. I don't think the trains are running tomorrow.

FIONA. Again?

How will you get to work?

STEPHEN. I don't think anyone's going in...

FIONA. You could walk...?

STEPHEN. No one wants to do that. Not with the roads in the state they're in...

FIONA. No...

STEPHEN. So I could make a start... clearing a bit of the garden...

FIONA. So we could see her better!

STEPHEN. Yes.

FIONA. If she's... around?

STEPHEN. Yes. She might not have gone so far.

FIONA. Might still be in the garden!

STEPHEN. Yes.

FIONA. But won't you... scare her... Mightn't that scare her away altogether?

STEPHEN. I don't know.

I need a scythe!

FIONA. I don't think they make them any more.

STEPHEN. If we don't cut some of this down, we won't be able to get out at all!

An animal call outside.

FIONA. Stephen... help me open the door...

STEPHEN. What's the point? What can you do?! You don't even know if it's her!

FIONA. I just want to call to her.

Another animal call.

Heavy, hurrying footsteps overhead.

STEPHEN. He's got a gun. If you call her out...

FIONA. He wouldn't do that.

STEPHEN. It's his garden now.

FIONA. He's still got kind eyes!

Kind, sad eyes.

He wouldn't.

We lived here together. We've trusted him. He wouldn't.

STEPHEN. He's frightened.

FIONA. We're all frightened!

Help me open the door.

He hesitates.

FIONA. I won't step out. I'll just call her.

He still hesitates.

She'll be frightened too, Stephen.

He helps her start to pull at the door. It's bolted, lots of locks. It's sticking with damp and pushing against undergrowth outside. They're struggling. It's open a crack. FIONA *calls out, quietly.*

Susan?

They wait, tense. Nothing.

(*Louder.*) Susan?

She edges out the door.

STEPHEN (*tense*). Not too far! Stay in the light. Stay close to the house!

FIONA (*outside*). Susan?

An animal howl/snarl close at hand, and then a deafening shot overhead.

FIONA *screams. She dives back into the house.* STEPHEN *slams the door. He locks every lock, bolts every bolt, feverish. Another howl, more distant, another shot.*

Oh God... Oh God... I couldn't see... I couldn't...

STEPHEN. Was it...? Was it her?

FIONA. I couldn't see?! I should have...

STEPHEN. No...

FIONA. I should have run out!

STEPHEN. No.

FIONA. I should have run after her! I should have...

STEPHEN. No. No. You have to stay here. We're safe here.

We're safe.

FIONA (*whisper*). Yes.

STEPHEN. We can't even be sure it was her.

FIONA. No.

STEPHEN. What can we do?

Pause.

Did he hit... whoever...?

FIONA. I don't know.

Pause.

STEPHEN. We'll have to let him build the fence. We have to.

FIONA *says nothing.*

What else can we do?

FIONA. We could...

We can't go out and find her... can we?

STEPHEN. How could we? How could anyone find her... out there... the way things are...

FIONA. No. No, we can't.

STEPHEN. He's hopeless. He's useless...

FIONA. He's dangerous, I never thought he'd do that, I never thought...

STEPHEN. 'Kind eyes'?!' He's scared out of his shoes...

FIONA. Yes...

STEPHEN. But it's his house. What can we do? We have to let him handle things his way.

FIONA. What else can we do?

Pause.

STEPHEN. I'll put the kettle on.

FIONA. Do we have herbal?

STEPHEN (*looks*). Lemon verbena.

FIONA. Oh.

Alright, I'll try that.

STEPHEN. I'll clear the path to the gate at least. You'll be able to get to the shops.

FIONA. Yes. That's a good idea.

Pause.

If we put her things in a box…

We will keep the box safe for her?

STEPHEN. If we can find a shelf away from the damp.

He's making tea. FIONA *looks at the ceiling.*

FIONA. All quiet now.

STEPHEN. Do you want me to talk to him?

FIONA. No. No, what good would it do?

STEPHEN. We're still better off than a lot of people. We're safe.

FIONA. Yes. We've got a roof over our heads. We're lucky.

STEPHEN. Yes.

Fade lights.

The End.

DISTRACTED

Morna Pearson

Morna Pearson is from Elgin, and currently lives in Edinburgh. Her first full professional production was *Distracted* at the Traverse Theatre in 2006. *Distracted* won the Meyer-Whitworth Award, was nominated for a CATS Award and was shortlisted for the Wolff-Whiting Award. Her other plays include: *Elf Analysis* (Òran Mór, Glasgow), *McBeth's McPets* (BBC Radio Scotland), *Side Effects* (BBC Radio 3 and Bona Broadcasting).

Distracted was first performed at the Traverse Theatre,
Edinburgh, on 31 October 2006, with the following cast:

JAMIE PURDY	Garry Collins
GEORGE-MICHAEL SKINNER	David Ireland
BUNNY SKINNER	Abigail Davies
GRANNY PURDY	Anne Lacey

Director	Lorne Campbell
Designer	Lisa Sangster
Lighting Designer	David Holmes

Characters

JAMIE PURDY, *thin and friendly looking. His clothes are dirty and are too small.*

GRANNY PURDY, *her clothes and skin are pale. She wears a pink cardigan and a tweed skirt. Jamie does not look directly at her.*

GEORGE-MICHAEL SKINNER, *he has grown up in the caravan park. He is a competent footballer and likes sportswear. He walks with a mild swagger.*

BUNNY SKINNER, *she became a mum in her teens. A Wham fan, she hosts a karaoke night at the local pub.*

Place

A small residential caravan park on the outskirts of a town in North East Scotland, close to a disused sand quarry and a small area of woodland. Day and night, the place is lively with the sounds of grasshoppers, cats fighting, dogs barking, motorbikes, drunks and music on Bunny Skinner's stereo.

Flower boxes line the outside of the Skinners' caravan. Occasionally there are empty milk bottles on the step, waiting for collection. The Purdys' caravan is dilapidated, inside is a lonely table and chair.

A blue-string washing line connects the two caravans. No blue set or costume, except props as specified.

Scene One

JAMIE PURDY *sits on the grass, fully absorbed with his pooter, empty milk bottles containing various dead insects and a notebook.* GEORGE-MICHAEL SKINNER *approaches with curiosity, a muddy football under his arm.*

GEORGE-MICHAEL. Hey, how's it goin?

JAMIE (*uncertain, he looks over his shoulder, then back to* GEORGE-MICHAEL). Fa, me?

GEORGE-MICHAEL. Aye you. Whit's all this?

JAMIE. This? It's a pooter.

GEORGE-MICHAEL. Looks very scientific.

JAMIE. It's actually a fairly basic method of collectin insects.

GEORGE-MICHAEL. Why wid you wint tae collect insects?

Long pause. He snatches the pooter from JAMIE *to examine it more closely.* GEORGE-MICHAEL *is suddenly not very interested and chucks it back to* JAMIE.

JAMIE. It's comprised of six parts. The plastic container. The magnified lid. The longer tube, to be placed over the insect. The shorter tube tae sook. And the gauze and lazzy band tae cover the base of the shorter tube so's you dinnae inhale your subject.

GEORGE-MICHAEL. Hm. Interesting. Let's see it at work then. Look, there's a wee slater.

JAMIE. Indeed, that's a woodlouse. Oniscus asellus.

GEORGE-MICHAEL. Whit?

JAMIE. Oniscus asellus.

GEORGE-MICHAEL. Whit?

JAMIE. Oniscus asellus.

GEORGE-MICHAEL. Hi-ya!

GEORGE-MICHAEL *karate hand-chops* JAMIE.

I'm George-Michael Skinner. I dinnae tak naen cheek.

JAMIE (*winded*). Girl's name.

GEORGE-MICHAEL. Whit?

JAMIE. That's a girl's name.

GEORGE-MICHAEL. Is it fuck! Get a grip. Jesus Christ –

JAMIE. Sorry, did I say girl's name? I meant it's a gay name.

GEORGE-MICHAEL. Hm.

Beat.

Hiv you jist moved in? It'll be great hivvin neighbours again after so long. That caravan's been empty for ages. The last family tae bide there were infested wi something or another. Environmental Health had tae chase them awa. Hopefully intae a sheep dip. But I spose the place has been cleaned up for you movin in.

JAMIE (*itching*). Aye.

GEORGE-MICHAEL. Me and my mither will be oota here soon. So, y'know, make the most of it. She's gonna be mair-rying an entrepreneur. Loaded. He's probably a total dick, like, but he's got a proper hoose wi stairs and everythin. And that's whit's important.

Pause.

D'you wint a game of fitba?

JAMIE. Dinnae play fitba.

GEORGE-MICHAEL. Hm.

Pause.

D'you wint tae play Grand Theft Auto?

JAMIE. Whit's that?

GEORGE-MICHAEL. D'you wint tae watch a video? We could watch *Jumanji*. It's my favourite.

JAMIE. Whit other videos dae you hiv?

GEORGE-MICHAEL. Just *Jumanji*.

JAMIE (*sighs*). Dunno…

GEORGE-MICHAEL. Hm. I'm starting tae think you dinnae hiv a personality.

Pause.

Whit's your suggestion?

JAMIE. Oh, um…

Beat.

Oh I ken! There's this really cool alphabet game –

GEORGE-MICHAEL. Alphabet game? Jesus Christ. Alphabet games are for losers. And naebiddy, but naebiddy, likes a loser.

Beat.

D'you wint tae stay at mine's for tea?

JAMIE. Aye, okay.

GEORGE-MICHAEL (*shouts unnecessarily loud*). Mum? Can – (*To* JAMIE.) whit's your name wee guv?

JAMIE. Jamie.

GEORGE-MICHAEL. Can Jamie stay for tea?

BUNNY (*inside caravan*). Whit?

GEORGE-MICHAEL. Can Jamie stay for tea!

BUNNY SKINNER *appears in the doorway, dressed in an apron and rubber gloves. As she lights a cigarette, she clocks* JAMIE.

BUNNY. Oh, hello.

GEORGE-MICHAEL. Mum, this is Jamie. Can he stay for tea?

BUNNY. Hello. Jamie.

JAMIE (*mumbles*). Hello, Mrs Sk –

BUNNY. Bunny. Ca' me Bunny. And I'm nae mairried.

Her look lingers.

Aye, alright. I've got a pie. It's big enough for ain mair.

(*To* GEORGE-MICHAEL.) Oh, Jamie'll love my pie, won't he, darling? (*To* JAMIE.) George-Michael loves his mammy's cookin. Cannae get enough. He's been fingerin my pie all afternoon.

GEORGE-MICHAEL. Mum.

BUNNY. Mind and wash your hands afore tea. You's boys aye hae sticky paws at your age.

GEORGE-MICHAEL. Mum.

BUNNY. A'wyes got his hands doon his draars this ain.

GEORGE-MICHAEL. Mum!

BUNNY *and* GEORGE-MICHAEL *playfully wrestle/hug as they enter the caravan.* JAMIE *reluctantly follows them until the blue washing line catches his eye. He runs a hand along it.*

Scene Two

The Purdys' caravan. JAMIE *sits at the table with his nose in his notebook. He has a milk bottle of insects on the table.* GRANNY PURDY *reads* Bella *magazine upside down.*

JAMIE. Three hunner and forty-seven. Three hunner and forty-eight. Three hunner and forty –

He sneezes into his notebook and knocks over the milk bottle.

Och min.

GRANNY. Whit a fanny.

JAMIE. Sorry.

GRANNY. Clean it up then. Dinnae wint beasties in our denner.

JAMIE (*scooping up mess*). Whit's for denner?

GRANNY (*contemplates*). Red sky at night – shepherd's pie.
Nae thit Granddad wid mind the beasties. He's eaten worse.

JAMIE. Far's Granddad?

GRANNY. In the war they had tae eat their ain shite. Let that
be a lesson tae you.

JAMIE. Far's Granddad?

GRANNY. Gone tae look for your mither. She's nae been
answering the phone.

Scene Three

Morning. JAMIE *steps out of his caravan and yawns.*
GEORGE-MICHAEL *suddenly appears.*

GEORGE-MICHAEL. Here, catch.

He throws a football to JAMIE. JAMIE *is startled and lets
the ball drop to the ground.*

Nice ain.

Fetches ball, then stands and stares at JAMIE.

Y'ken, I dinnae jist play fitba. I can dae other stuff.

JAMIE. Okay.

GEORGE-MICHAEL. I can put up a tent. When me and Mum
go camping we mak up these futuristic nature dances of the
future.

Pause.

D'you wint tae see ain?

Silence.

JAMIE. Okay.

GEORGE-MICHAEL (*dancing*). We call that ain 'The Robotic Ginger Squirrel Scavenging For Nuts But Some of the Nuts are Bombs'.

Still looking for a reaction.

Y'ken footballers use the same muscles as ballet dancers. So...

Beat.

Y'ken, Jamie, after staying tea most folk would say thanks. And double flush.

Silence.

Are you here wi your mum and dad?

JAMIE. Granny. I'm wi my granny.

GEORGE-MICHAEL. Far's your mum and dad, like?

JAMIE *barely shrugs.*

Weel, I ken some dads can fuck off, but you must've come ooto some wifie's fanny.

JAMIE. Umm...

GEORGE-MICHAEL (*shouts*). Mum! Jamie disnae hiv a mum or dad!

BUNNY *appears in the doorway, stretches and yawns.*

BUNNY. But you must've come ooto some wifie's fanny.

GEORGE-MICHAEL (*chuffed*). That's whit I said!

BUNNY. Dinnae you hiv ony memories, Jamie? Nae recollections?

JAMIE *is very uncomfortable.*

I see. Naen nice enough tae remember.

She puts her arm around him.

Y'ken when I wis wee… I had a tough time. I mean, tae look at me noo you wouldnae think it, but, oh Jamie, I had a terrible time. The things I saw, nae child should see. The drunken arguments, the threatening stares, the scruciating silences, the smashed plates and glass, the violent beatings. I'd be huddled in a corner, wi my fingers in my ears and my eyes tight shut, wishing it would stop. But every night. The humiliation. The brutality. The cruel sexual games.

Pause.

And my dad, he jist took it.

Pause.

And the wish, the need, tae block it oot has always been there.

Beat.

You must hiv some memories, Jamie. Are you fae roon here?

GEORGE-MICHAEL. Are you fae the toon?

BUNNY. Maybe I went tae school wi your parents.

GEORGE-MICHAEL. Aye, Mum kens a cunts.

BUNNY (*skelps* GEORGE-MICHAEL*'s head*). Language, you dirty wee shite.

JAMIE. There is somebiddy. A manny.

GEORGE-MICHAEL. Your dad?

BUNNY *and* GEORGE-MICHAEL *move in closer in anticipation.*

JAMIE. He has the skin of an itchy bastard. The reflection of deep-fried penguins in his eyes. His hair moves like a jellyfish and his purse is made of cheese. His elbows are chapped and leaking. He's a septic mess.

Silence. BUNNY *and* GEORGE-MICHAEL *pull back, exchange a glance.*

BUNNY. Och weel, each tae their ain.

Scene Four

GRANNY *munches her way through a packet of Rich Tea biscuits by the end of the scene. However, she does not swallow but lets the biscuits fall from her mouth onto the floor.*

GRANNY. Wint a biscuit?

JAMIE. Whit kind?

GRANNY. Rich Tea.

JAMIE. Oh. Got any Jammie Dodgers?

GRANNY. Don't be fucking stupid. The jam sticks to my dentures.

JAMIE. Okay.

GRANNY. Come and gie your granny a hug.

JAMIE. Umm…

GRANNY. I put this cardigan on specially. That's what we grannies do. We wrap ourselves up in pink fluffy cardigans to make it a little easier for you to hug the rattling death that is Granny.

JAMIE. I've got a sore heed.

GRANNY. D'you wint granny to tuck you into bed and give you a pill to make your nasty headache go away? A sugar-coated pill. Maks everything a little easier to swallow, doesn't it?

JAMIE. I wint tae go oot tae play.

GRANNY. Well, come and gie your granny a kiss then. It's a shame aboot Granny's arsehole breath, isn't it? We do try to disguise the smell with Dundee Cake. We do try.

JAMIE. Eh, I'll jist have a Rich Tea, thanks.

GRANNY. You cannae. They're all gone.

Scene Five

Midnight. BUNNY *leans against her door frame, smoking. She holds a bunch of chive flowers in one hand.* JAMIE *opens his door. As he takes a step out he notices* BUNNY. *He swiftly steps back in and shuts the door.*

BUNNY. Hi, Jamie.

Pause.

Jamie?

Pause.

Jamie, I saw you.

JAMIE *reluctantly opens his door and steps outside. He tries to avoid eye contact.*

A bitty late tae be oot, is it nae?

JAMIE. Just goin for a walk.

BUNNY. I widnae dae that, deary. It's nae safe. Night-time's when all the wierdos come oot.

Inhales/exhales.

Like me.

Pause.

But, seriously, there's a heap of drunks aboot here. The police hiv shunted them oot of the toon centre. So they've flit tae here. The bit far naebiddy gies twa shites aboot. We could be on a tiny rock. Floating in space.

JAMIE. Okay.

BUNNY *stubs her cigarette out with her foot.*

BUNNY. I host a karaoke night. Did George-Michael tell you that? Eighties music mostly. Bit o Wham, Bangles, Milli Vanilli. You should come doon ain night. We could dae a duet. Whit aboot Elton John? D'you like Elton?

JAMIE. Fa?

BUNNY. 'Saturday Nicht's Alricht for Fichting'?

JAMIE. Pardon?

BUNNY (*sings*). Coz Saturday nicht's the nicht I like, Saturday nicht's alricht alricht alricht, ooh!

JAMIE feels uncomfortable. BUNNY sighs.

Japan is but a dream. My Karen Carpenter, wi their state-of-the-art equipment. I tell you. Wid bring tears tae their wee faces. Tears.

BUNNY peers into her caravan and shuts the door.

Oh, we better nae disturb George-Michael. He's hivvin his bedtime wank. He has trouble sleeping. Poor wee manny. But after a wee tug he's off like a baby. I like tae gie him a bit o privacy, y'ken. Does your granny dae the same wi you?

JAMIE. Um.

BUNNY. I should ask your granny roon for a cup o tea ain day. Bet she's git some stories aboot you.

JAMIE. Um. You're getting mairried.

BUNNY. Oh, is that whit George-Michael telt you?

Pause.

Well, maybes I am. D'you like my flowers? Fae lover-boy.

She winks. Lights a cigarette.

You dinnae smoke, dae you?

JAMIE. No.

BUNNY. Good boy. I nivver smoke indoors. Least then naebiddy can accuse me of damaging my son. Least nae physically.

Pause.

And I try nae tae smile when I've got a fag in my hand either. I dinnae wint tae glamorise it.

She winks. JAMIE *smiles nervously.*

Scene Six

Morning. JAMIE *sits on the grass examining a quadrat, with a notebook in hand.* GEORGE-MICHAEL *stands in the doorway of his caravan in his pyjamas. He yawns and stretches conspicuously. His attention quickly transfers to* JAMIE.

GEORGE-MICHAEL. Well, Jesus, Jamie and Joseph – whit hiv you got noo?

Without looking up, JAMIE *holds a hand up to silence* GEORGE-MICHAEL *for a very long time until he's finished what he's doing, then looks up with a smile.*

JAMIE. Morning, George.

GEORGE-MICHAEL. George-*Michael*. It's hyphenated. Get it right.

JAMIE. Okay.

GEORGE-MICHAEL *has two blue bags of crisps, he chucks one to* JAMIE.

GEORGE-MICHAEL. Here. Crisps.

Starts eating his crisps until JAMIE'*s following actions catch his attention.*

JAMIE *is taken aback, he stares at the crisps, slowly reaches to pick up the packet, examines it, sniffs it, slowly opens it, peers in, shuffles it, rakes around a bit, turns the packet upside down, watches the crisps all fall out onto the quadrat, peers into the empty packet, finally drops it on the ground.*

Carries on as normal…

JAMIE. Bin daein quadrat surveys all morning. Y'ken, checking for the abundance of plants and animals and that. I've done six. All ower the caravan park. The results are pretty interesting. For every metre-squared area of grass in this park there's – wait for it – eighteen-and-a-half daisies, forty-seven clovers, five dandelions, four dock leaves a forkie, eight ants, thirteen fag ends, a third of a Special Brew can, one-sixth of a syringe – used – one-sixth of a sanitary towel – unused, phew – two-thirds of a rabbit –

GEORGE-MICHAEL. A rabbit? That's unexpected.

JAMIE. Aye, it followed me for four quadrats. Oh and, one, two, three, four, five…

Counts the crisps and mumbles to himself.

Divided by six, equals…

Deeply exhales.

Did you ken there's raspberries growin ower there.

GEORGE-MICHAEL. Aye. They belong tae the farmer fa owns the wids.

JAMIE. Oh.

Pause.

And I found some other things of interest. Look at this leaf. There's seventy-three aphids on jist this ain leaf. Eriosoma lanigerum.

GEORGE-MICHAEL. Okay, Harry Potter.

JAMIE. And look whit else.

Holds up a small green branch.

Cuckoo spit! There's tons of it ower there.

GEORGE-MICHAEL. Whit is it?

JAMIE. It's froth that baby froghoppers produce tae protect themsel's fae predators and fae goin crispy.

GEORGE-MICHAEL. Is it real spit? Certainly looks lik real gobbins.

He touches the froth.

JAMIE. No, comes fae its anus.

GEORGE-MICHAEL. Aw, man!

Wipes his fingers on JAMIE*'s top.*

Whit are you daein all this shit for onywye? I dinnae understand it. Why d'you hae tae mak lists and collect all the wee pishy beasties in bottles? Whit are you actually looking for? And how come you dinnae ken whit a PlayStation is? Eh? Are you fae the country like?

JAMIE. No, I… jist like countin things. Wallpaper wi hunners of stars on it. Dunno. Keeps my mind off things.

Stuffs all the crisps from the ground into his mouth.

GEORGE-MICHAEL. Keeps your mind off things? Whit things? How old are you? Whit kind of things does your mind hae on it? 'Cept for fitba, quinies, new trainers, Scrumpy Jack, computers –

A roar comes from several motorbikes not far in the distance. JAMIE *suddenly stops chewing.*

JAMIE. Whit's the noise?

GEORGE-MICHAEL. Motorbikes.

JAMIE. I dinnae like it.

GEORGE-MICHAEL. Well, get used tae it, coz they go up tae the wids all the time. They've bin daein it since they wis teenagers, supposedly. Tae smoke dope and tae shoot squirrels. Noo they probably jist go up tae bum each other. Or bum the squirrels. Whit is the world coming tae, ay.

Shakes his head.

Y'ken, Jamie, you've nivver asked me aboot my dad.

Pause.

D'you wint tae ask me aboot my dad?

JAMIE. Um, s'pose. Whit aboot your dad?

Beat.

Did he die shortly after mating wi your mither?

They laugh.

GEORGE-MICHAEL. Aye.

JAMIE. Did she eat him up and shite oot his bones and feathers?

They laugh.

GEORGE-MICHAEL. Aye.

JAMIE. Did she inject a digestive juice intae his cephalothorax and abdomen and suck up his fluid remains?

JAMIE *laughs.*

GEORGE-MICHAEL. Nut. He's yin of they bikers.

JAMIE. Okay.

GEORGE-MICHAEL. But I dinnae ken whit ain. The day I asked my mum fa my dad wis she jist pointed tae the bikers, fa were going up the track, and said him. They wis going so fast I didnae catch whit ain she meant.

Pause.

I'm nae sure she kent hersel. She had a tear in her eye.

JAMIE. Got ony mair crisps?

GEORGE-MICHAEL. Sometimes I go up tae where they've been, tae look for clues in the rubbish they've left. And ain time I stood at the side of the track and waited for them all tae go past so's I could look them all in the eyes. See if I could recognise my dad, or he me. But nothing. I couldnae tell. Jist hope it's nae the mental ain.

JAMIE. Mental ain?

GEORGE-MICHAEL. Aye. Ain of them had flippin crazy eyes. I hope he's nae my dad.

JAMIE. Crazy eyes?

GEORGE-MICHAEL. I can tell by looking at somebiddy, within a split second, whether they're a normal or a mental. It's their eyes, y'see. It's my gift.

JAMIE (*averting his eyes*). But you're getting a new dad, ay?

GEORGE-MICHAEL. Aye, s'pose. I hope he's nice.

JAMIE. Hiv you nae met him?

GEORGE-MICHAEL. Nut, but my mum's telt me all aboot him. He's an entrepreneur, did I tell you? He's launching a new brand of cider, called Golden Shower. I've tried it. It's quite nice.

Pause.

It's aimed at the cheap end of the market. Alchies and teenagers. So it'll make a mint. Though I think he's already loaded, coz Mum says he's given her a pearl necklace on many an occasion.

JAMIE. Hmm.

GEORGE-MICHAEL. Hmm whit?

JAMIE. He gied your mum chives and called them flowers.

GEORGE-MICHAEL. Whit of it?

JAMIE. Just sayin. A chive's a herb.

GEORGE-MICHAEL. Whit the fuck's that supposed tae mean?

Long silence. JAMIE *scribbles in his notebook.*

Look, I'm sorry, Jamie. D'you like apples?

Affectionately nudges him.

D'you wint an apple?

JAMIE. Um, okay.

GEORGE-MICHAEL. S'pose you ken heaps aboot apples, ay? Like you ken heaps aboot insects and that.

JAMIE. Aye, sort of.

GEORGE-MICHAEL. Whit's your favourite?

JAMIE. Apple? I'm nae fussy. Braeburn s'pose.

GEORGE-MICHAEL. I'm afraid we've naen Braeburn.

Beat.

We've only got them ains thit begin with C.

Beat.

D'you like them ains thit begin with C? You'll ken whit they're called…

JAMIE. Cox. Aye, I like Cox.

GEORGE-MICHAEL (*shouts*). Mum! Jamie said he likes cocks!

He laughs. BUNNY *pops her head out the door.*

Mum, Jamie said he likes cocks!

He laughs.

BUNNY. I thought I telt you tae bring in the milk!

GEORGE-MICHAEL. There's naen! Look!

BUNNY. Weel, get some claes on. You're goin tae the shoppy.

GEORGE-MICHAEL *sulks into the caravan.*

Guid mornin, Jamie. I hear we've got something in common.

She winks, then shuts the door. JAMIE *is left confused.*

Scene Seven

The Purdys' caravan. JAMIE *sits at the table with an empty glass in front of him.*

JAMIE. George-Michael wis a bit angry the day.

GRANNY. It's come as no surprise.

JAMIE. He didnae ask me ower for tea.

GRANNY. She wis nivver a happy lassie.

JAMIE. Bunny keeps winking at me.

GRANNY. There's nae easy wye tae tell you this, Jamie.

JAMIE. As if she kens something.

GRANNY. But your mummy's gone.

JAMIE. Can you pass the milk, please.

GRANNY. Your mummy's dead.

JAMIE. Can you pass the milk, please.

GRANNY. She's dead.

> GRANNY *puts a bottle of milk on the table.*

JAMIE. Thank you.

GRANNY. Shh. There, there.

> JAMIE *tips the bottle towards the glass. White pills spill out. He is shaken.*

> Shh. There, there. Your granddad is wi her noo. Found her slumped ower in the bath.

JAMIE (*stutters as he begins to count the pills*). One, t-two, three, four –

GRANNY. Skin wis purple.

JAMIE. – thirteen, fourteen, fifteen, sixteen –

GRANNY. Eyes open. Lips blue.

JAMIE. – twenty, twenty-one, twenty-two –

GRANNY. Drip drip drip. Her hair still wet.

JAMIE. Twenty-six, twenty-seven, twenty-eight –

GRANNY. It's come as no surprise.

JAMIE. Thirty-two, thirty-three, thirty-four –

GRANNY. Doctors said it wis inevitable. She wis nivver a happy lassie.

JAMIE. I've lost count…

GRANNY. Became worse wi your faither gone.

JAMIE. I've lost count…

He begins to count again silently.

GRANNY. She believed in love at first sight. Said she widnae waste time wi onything less than a soulmate.

Pause.

She found him, on Ward Four.

Pause.

As crazy as each other.

Pause.

After your faither disappeared

When I arrived at your hoose

She didnae ken how long he'd been gone

You were crawling

In two weeks of faeces

Your mither

In a corner

Shaking

Crying

In between gasps for air

Spoke tae the chicken on the packet

Asked the flakes of corn

Far her lover had gone.

JAMIE has stopped counting. He is breathing heavily.

JAMIE (*whispers*). Far had daddy gone?

GRANNY. A waster

A hippy

Thought he'd fled tae the Foundation

Until we found him

Twa children found him

Washed up on Primrose Bay

He wis naked

Self-mutilated

On your first birthday.

Scene Eight

The next day. JAMIE *lays on the grass.*

JAMIE (*sighs*). Observing change. It's interesting how things change. Change. Move. Grow. Bigger. Smaller. Colour. Open. Close. Multiply. Bloom. Pale. Disappear. Disappear.

Beat.

Disappear.

GEORGE-MICHAEL *swings from his doorframe, jumps to the ground.*

GEORGE-MICHAEL. Hey wee guv. Fa you talkin tae?

JAMIE. Um, I wis jist reciting nouns of animal congregations. A smack of jellyfish. A flange of baboons. A peep of chickens. A parcel of penguins.

GEORGE-MICHAEL. Aye, whitever. (*Wiping his mouth on his sleeve.*) Dinnae you hate it when your mither sees you've git a dirty face, but instead of saying 'you've git a dirty face' she says 'come here' and afore you ken it she's licked her thumb and wiped it on your mooth.

JAMIE. Aye.

GEORGE-MICHAEL. It's disgusting. And then the smell of her mingin saliva is stuck ontae your face.

JAMIE. Aye.

GEORGE-MICHAEL. Specially if she smokes.

JAMIE. Aye.

GEORGE-MICHAEL. Stinks.

Pause.

D'you wint a three-legged race?

JAMIE. D'you hiv a tie?

GEORGE-MICHAEL. Eh, whit aboot a wheelbarrow race?

JAMIE. Jist oursels?

GEORGE-MICHAEL. Least we'll always win.

JAMIE. Aye, okay.

GEORGE-MICHAEL. You be the wheelbarrow.

JAMIE *gets on all-fours,* GEORGE-MICHAEL *lifts* JAMIE*'s legs by holding on to his upper thighs.*

BUNNY (*popping her head out of the caravan*). Hey, boys… um…whit on earth…

GEORGE-MICHAEL. Wheelbarrow race.

BUNNY. Oh right. I wis wondering if you's fancy goin tae the beach the day?

GEORGE-MICHAEL. Aye, that's mair fun.

He quite brutally lets go of JAMIE*'s legs.* JAMIE *lands flat on the ground.*

BUNNY. Jamie?

JAMIE (*in pain*). Aye, beach is cool.

Getting up.

Oh, I dinnae hiv trunks. Or a towel. Or a bucket. Or a spade.

BUNNY. That's okay. Strange, but okay. You can borrow his fitba shorts.

GEORGE-MICHAEL. Mum!

BUNNY *glares at him*.

Weel, nae skidmarks, mind.

JAMIE. I love the beach. Better tak my notebook. There's goin tae be heaps of stuff, winkles, hermit crabs, jellyfish, sea anemone, limpets, urchins, starfish. If you rip a leg off a starfish, and provided at least a fifth of the central disc is still attached, that leg will grow intae a complete starfish again!

BUNNY. You're a fountain of knowledge, Jamie.

GEORGE-MICHAEL. Last time Mum wis at the beach all she caught wis crabs.

He laughs.

BUNNY. And you're a fountain of shite.

Beat.

I thought we could go tae that nice sandy beach wi the cliffs.

GEORGE-MICHAEL. Primrose Bay?

BUNNY. Aye. Primrose Bay.

JAMIE. Primrose Bay?

He hyperventilates and vomits into his cupped hands.

GEORGE-MICHAEL. Man alive.

BUNNY. Oh, for fuck's sake.

Scene Nine

Ten minutes later. JAMIE *and* GEORGE-MICHAEL *stand in their trunks next to a kid's paddling pool.* BUNNY *pours a final bucket of water into it, a cigarette hangs out of her mouth.*

BUNNY. Richt, that's as deep as it gets coz there's a huge fag burn there. Hop in.

> BUNNY *and* JAMIE *quickly sit in the pool. There is clearly no room for* GEORGE-MICHAEL. *He sits on his steps and watches them in a huff.*

Ooh, it's a bit nippy.

JAMIE. Aye. Brrr.

BUNNY. So, whit dae we dae noo? Jist sit here?

GEORGE-MICHAEL *(to himself)*. We could go tae the fucking beach.

JAMIE. Um, we could play this really cool alphabet game.

GEORGE-MICHAEL *(to himself)*. As if.

JAMIE. Whit we dae is starting wi A, we tak it in turns tae name a living creature. And the first ain tae pass or pause for too long gets splashed. Then we move on tae B and so on.

BUNNY *(stubbing out her cigarette on the ground)*. Sounds like fun.

GEORGE-MICHAEL *(under his breath)*. Get a room.

BUNNY. I'll stairt. Ant.

JAMIE. Anteater.

BUNNY. Antelope.

JAMIE. Aphid.

BUNNY. Um… eh…

JAMIE. Too late!

He splashes BUNNY. *She squeals. They laugh.* GEORGE-MICHAEL *sighs and rolls his eyes.*

GEORGE-MICHAEL. Now B. You hiv tae start.

BUNNY. B. A bee!

JAMIE. Butterfly.

BUNNY. Badger.

JAMIE. Beetle.

BUNNY. Bat.

JAMIE. Bison.

BUNNY. Bear.

JAMIE. Badger.

BUNNY. Said it!

JAMIE stares at her as she laughs, splashes him, throws her head back and laughs. GEORGE-MICHAEL *tuts and shakes his head.*

JAMIE. *One.*

BUNNY. Bat.

JAMIE. Bison.

BUNNY. Bear.

JAMIE. Badger.

BUNNY. Said it!

JAMIE stares at her as she laughs, splashes him, throws her head back and laughs. GEORGE-MICHAEL *tuts and shakes his head.*

JAMIE. *Two.*

BUNNY. Bat.

JAMIE. Bison.

BUNNY. Bear.

JAMIE. Badger.

BUNNY. Said it!

> JAMIE *stares at her as she laughs, splashes him, throws her head back and laughs.* GEORGE-MICHAEL *tuts and shakes his head.*

JAMIE. *Three.*

> BUNNY*'s hearty laugh turns into a hideous smoker's cough. She hacks up phlegm and spits it into the pool.*

BUNNY (*lifting herself out of the pool*). Hing on a wee minty. I'll get another fag. Then we can get ontae C.

> *She chuckles.*

Scene Ten

JAMIE *peers out of his ajar caravan door. He watches* GEORGE-MICHAEL *fasten his football boots, then exit. Meanwhile,* BUNNY *is aggressively tending to the flower boxes. She's very focused and serious, a disturbingly different mood from how we've seen her before.* JAMIE *sticks his head right out to check for the all-clear. He tiptoes out, rubs dirt from the ground onto his face, then stands closely behind* BUNNY. *It's a while before she notices him.*

BUNNY (*startled*). Jamie –

> *Her mood begins to soften.*

JAMIE. Is George-Michael in?

BUNNY. No, he isnae. Can I help?

JAMIE. No, nae really. I wis jist wintin tae tell him…

> *Pause.*

I says the aphids wis eriosoma lanigerum, but I wis wrong.
Brevicoryne brassicae is whit they are.

BUNNY. I'll nivver remember that, Jamie.

JAMIE. It's probably nae important.

Pause.

I'll jist sit here and wait for him.

Sits close to BUNNY.

Snakes hiv nae eyelids but their pupil is vertically slit so
closes tae keep the sun oot.

BUNNY. Eh?

JAMIE (*fiddles with* BUNNY*'s shoelaces*). Hiv you ever seen a
four-leafed clover? I have. It wisnae mine, it wis somebiddy
else's. Somebiddy else's luck. (*Nervous laugh.*) Far did you
say he wis?

BUNNY. I think he took his fitba oot tae the field.

Sits beside him.

You could join him. I think he'd really appreciate it. He disnae
hiv onybiddy tae kick aboot wi these days. Nae men in his life.
'Cept his uncle, of course. But he cannae coz he's blind.

JAMIE. That's a shame for him, being blind. Got any crisps?

BUNNY. Och no, dinnae feel sorry for him. He's hivvin a
whale of a time at the minute. He's git quinies trippin ower
themsels tae help him across the street. Nivver been happier.

Beat.

He's a very sexual being. Very sexual.

Beat.

Oh aye, you'd get on wi him fine. He keeps exotic pets.
Terrapins, a gecko, twa bearded lizards and a couple of they
avocados. They dinnae dae much. They jist sit in a bowl.

Noticing JAMIE*'s face.*

Och, Jamie, yiv git dirt aroon your mooth.

JAMIE (*knowingly*). Oh. Do I?

BUNNY (*licks her thumb*). Come here, mucky pup.

Wiping his mouth. JAMIE *smiles.*

So... George-Michael mentioned aboot me getting mairried.

JAMIE. Aye.

BUNNY. And whit else has he said?

JAMIE. Jist that he's an entrepreneur and yous are movin intae his hoose wi stairs and everything.

BUNNY. Shite.

She bites her nails.

JAMIE. Biting your nails.

BUNNY (*becoming upset*). He's nae real.

JAMIE. Your eyes are wet.

BUNNY. I made him up.

JAMIE (*clicks his fingers and points*). So's you didnae get chives as flowers.

BUNNY. Ain night he seen me kissing a manny ootside. I didnae wint him tae think his mammy wis a tart, so I telt him that me and this manny wis in a relationship. I'd really jist met him that night in the pub. I started telling George-Michael wee things aboot him. You ken when you say pretend words and George-Michael's in his pyjamas.

Beat.

Bedtime stories. But I've got a gob on me when I'm drunk though, and I think I took it a bit far. I thought that by the time I wid hiv tae show proper evidence of this boyfriend I'd hiv found a real relationship. I mean, that's nae much tae ask, is it? I'm nae that ugly, am I? But no. I've fucked up.

JAMIE. *Bat.*

BUNNY. *Bison.*

JAMIE. *Bear*.

BUNNY. *Badger*.

JAMIE. *Said it*.

BUNNY. I mean, I could jist tell him. But I cannae take the stories away frae him. Withoot the stories we hiv nothing.

Pause.

I feel like we've got tae get oota here. I feel like there's a big plastic bag ower the caravan park. But the park's actually a head. A huge breathing head. And wi every breath the bag gets tighter –

JAMIE. *Bat*.

BUNNY. *Bison*.

JAMIE. *Bear*.

BUNNY. *Bruised*.

JAMIE. *Said it*.

BUNNY. Suffocating. That's whit's happening. Being suffocated. And it's nae like we can move. We cannae afford tae.

Continuous sound of motorbikes in the distance.

Oh God. I wish they'd leave me the fuck alane. The mannies on the bikes. They keep tormenting me. For years they've bin tormenting me. I feel like I'm part of a crazy game. I may be the ain rolling the dice but I dinnae hiv control ower the ootcome whitsoever. Hiv you seen *Jumanji*?

JAMIE. *Bat*.

BUNNY. *Bison*.

JAMIE. *Bear*.

BUNNY. *Blood*.

JAMIE. *Said it*.

BUNNY. I wis just sixteen. I lived here. I used tae play up in they wids. Myself, I didnae hiv friends. I'd usually take string and a penknife so's I could make a bow and arrow. But on this day I wis jist climbing trees. I could hear a motorbike approaching, but then silence. I slid down the trunk and as my feet landed a hand touched my back. I turned, seen his face and screamed.

JAMIE. *Bat*.

BUNNY. *Bison*.

JAMIE. *Bear*.

BUNNY. *Bath*.

JAMIE. *Said it*.

BUNNY. He bit my lip. The stench of his rotting teeth. He began to touch me, the roar of motorbikes drooned oot my cries. Naebiddy could hear me scream! Blood and fluid running down my legs! Naebiddy answered my scream!

Crying, she hugs JAMIE. *Silence*.

I'm afraid. Jamie. I might snap. Jamie. I might start walking. And nae turn back.

Silence.

JAMIE. Moles munch doon worms heed-first so all the shite squishes oot.

Long silence. BUNNY *begins to laugh*.

BUNNY (*having perked up*). So, you dinnae play fitba?

JAMIE. That's right.

BUNNY. You're mair intae animals.

JAMIE. Aye.

BUNNY. Whit d'you think aboot birds?

JAMIE. Quite like them, nae as much as mammals though.

BUNNY. Whit wid you say if I telt you I had a pair of great tits, and that I wint tae show you them?

JAMIE. Great tits? Two? Far?

BUNNY (*nods to caravan*). In here.

JAMIE. Wow. They usually feed in the wids at this time of year. So, seeing them in the gairden wid be pretty amazing. But in a caravan – that's unprecedented!

BUNNY *giggles and goes into the caravan.*

I'll get my notebook!

He runs to fetch it. GEORGE-MICHAEL *enters.*

GEORGE-MICHAEL. Whit's all the rush?

JAMIE. Your mum's goin tae show me her tits!

He rushes past and into the caravan. The door shuts. Long silence. GEORGE-MICHAEL *looks at the door expectantly, with one hand on his hip, the other holding a football. The door opens.* JAMIE *slowly steps out, his eyes and mouth are wide open. He is speechless. He closes the door.*

GEORGE-MICHAEL. So. Did you tak notes?

JAMIE. Nut.

GEORGE-MICHAEL. Did you draw a diagram, ay?

JAMIE. Nut.

GEORGE-MICHAEL. Here, hiv I got shit on my back?

Turning back to JAMIE.

JAMIE. Nut, eh, aye, a wee bit.

GEORGE-MICHAEL. I wis playing shit-stick wi Neep and he caught me, the dirty bastard.

JAMIE. Fa's Neep?

GEORGE-MICHAEL. He's a tramp. Hiv you nae seen him aboot? We're great pals. Nae at first though. I set fire tae him. Thought he wis deed, like. I'm nae that seek tae set fire tae a livin tramp, am I? But he wis actually sleeping. So's he stairts screaming and shouting. And I panicked. The only thing I could think tae dae wis piss on him tae put the flames oot. His face and beard got the main damage though coz I couldnae piss on his face. That wid be insulting.

JAMIE. That's really…

GEORGE-MICHAEL. S'pose it wis, aye.

Pause.

Tramps burn well. Nae much smoke. It's all that dry crusty claes.

Looks at watch.

Och weel, Mum should hiv her top back on. Better show her the damage tae my T-shirt. See you later.

JAMIE. Aye, see you.

JAMIE *stares at the flower box* BUNNY *was digging. It has two bright blue flowers in it. He picks off the two flower heads, holds them up to his eyes, then puts them in his pocket. He begins to dig with his hands to the bottom of the flower box. Frustrated, he tips the box upside down, shakes it empty, looks inside it. He is disappointed.*

Scene Eleven

JAMIE *sits at the table with his head in his hands.*

JAMIE. Holy moly. Whit a fix.

Pause.

That's whit you say, Granny, ay? Holy moly, whit a fix. Go and say it.

GRANNY. Mm. D'you wint my advice? You should put an end tae it all.

JAMIE. You're right –

GRANNY. D'you ken whit your Great-Uncle Billy wid say at a time like this?

JAMIE. Great-Uncle Billy?

GRANNY. Mind. Hair like a jellyfish, purse made of cheese...

JAMIE. Oh aye.

GRANNY. Well, Great-Uncle Billy wid say smash the bottle, stab it intae your face.

JAMIE. Noo, Granny, that's hardly goin tae solve the problem wi the Skinners, is it?

GRANNY. Whit's the problem?

JAMIE. Well, Bunny telt me stuff. And I dinnae ken if I should tell George-Michael.

GRANNY. So, whit's the problem?

JAMIE. George-Michael's my friend. My best friend.

GRANNY. Your only friend.

JAMIE. My *best* only friend.

GRANNY. The rabbits wid hiv something tae say aboot this.

JAMIE. The whit?

GRANNY. The rabbits wid tell you tae get the cable from George-Michael's PlayStation and wrap it roon your neck.

JAMIE. The whit, Granny?

GRANNY. Take ten too many Prozac.

JAMIE. Prozac?

GRANNY. You'd recognise the taste of it. Your mither's milk wis full of it.

JAMIE. No.

Covers his ears and counts silently.

GRANNY. That's whit you'd dae in your mither's womb. You'd hiv your fingers in your ears and you'd be counting. Counting the number of punches your mither threw at you. Coz the larger you grew, the love she got fae your faither got smaller.

A picture falls off the wall.

There's nae greater wye tae achieve absolution, than watching the life flow oot of your wrists.

Another picture falls off the wall.

Somebiddy get me a damp clooty, coz I'm on fire.

Scene Twelve

JAMIE *sits on his step. His quadrat lies on the ground. He is bloated and has raspberries on his face and fingers.* GEORGE-MICHAEL *approaches.*

GEORGE-MICHAEL. Hey, badger-bum. How's it going?

JAMIE (*grins*). I've been pickin raspberries.

GEORGE-MICHAEL. No shit.

JAMIE (*burps*). I feel a bit seek though.

GEORGE-MICHAEL. So, Jamie. Do you like milk?

JAMIE. Aye. Love it. Why?

Beat.

Uh-oh, this isn't another trick far I say I like milk and then you tak me intae your caravan and show me your –

GEORGE-MICHAEL. Hiv you noticed that oot of all the caravans here, yours is the only ain that disnae get milk delivered.

JAMIE. Aye?

GEORGE-MICHAEL. Aye. And milk's been disappearing ever since you arrived.

JAMIE. Aye?

GEORGE-MICHAEL. Aye. But I see you've got plenty empty bottles.

JAMIE. My granny gets the milk.

GEORGE-MICHAEL. Really?

JAMIE. Aye.

GEORGE-MICHAEL. Weel, I'll hiv tae ask her far she gets it.

He reaches for the door, but JAMIE *stands in his way. They struggle.*

JAMIE. No! Stop it!

GEORGE-MICHAEL. Move!

JAMIE. You cannae see her!

GEORGE-MICHAEL. Move!

JAMIE. She's asleep... she's ill... she's deaf... she bites!

GEORGE-MICHAEL *backs off. He is suspicious.*

GEORGE-MICHAEL.Weel... jist watch it. I'm watching you. So, watch oot.

As he leaves, he stamps on JAMIE*'s quadrat. It breaks.* JAMIE *rushes to assess the damage. In a rage he throws it to the ground, then kicks the side of the caravan. He hurts his foot. He limps up the step into his caravan.*

Scene Thirteen

The Purdys' caravan. Silence. JAMIE *and* GRANNY *both sneeze at the same time.*

JAMIE (*quietly*). You're still here.

Pause.

Right then. Far are you? You wint tae hiv a go as well?

Silence.

I've had enough. Far are you? I'm back tae the sick teeth of this!

Silence. He breathes heavily. He turns to the small dirty window. Cleans a section of it with his fingers and presses his nose to it.

There she is. Hinging oot the washing. Her soft skin.

Beat.

She smiled. She splashed me. She threw her heed back and laughed.

Beat.

The water drip-dripped off her hair.

Beat.

A light that I'm drawn tae.

Pause.

Wint her tae touch me.

GRANNY. Pervert.

JAMIE. There you go.

GRANNY. Pervert.

JAMIE. Nae like that. I wint her tae touch – cuddle – me, like mummies dae.

GRANNY. Pussy.

JAMIE. Maybe that's how she winks. She taken it the wrong wye.

GRANNY. Pervert.

JAMIE. Alright, that's enough. Jist get it off your chest.

Silence.

Tell me everything. Give me everything you've got. I can handle it.

Silence.

Come on then. Jist get it off your wheezy chest. Jist whit is it you've got tae say?

GRANNY *makes false crying/whimpering sounds.*

Oh, I'm sorry I –

GRANNY (*back with aggression*). Pervert.

JAMIE. You're nae talking like a granny. Bunny disnae speak tae George-Michael like that.

GRANNY. Tell me, Jamie, hiv you seen the rabbits yet? Hiv you seen the rabbits?

JAMIE. I saw a rabbit the other day.

GRANNY. I kent it.

JAMIE. It followed my quadrat.

GRANNY. I kent you'd seen the rabbits. Jist like your mither.

JAMIE. I seen jist ain rabbit.

GRANNY. Jist like your mither. She seen the rabbits. The rabbits wi naen fur. Skint. Red and raw flesh. Said they'd chase her roon her room. A hale troop of rabbits.

JAMIE. Colony.

GRANNY. The skinny beasts wid chase her roon, shouting, we're gonna eat your face off. We're gonna bite and scratch your face off and leave your eyes till last so's you can see it all happening. And she'd be clawing at the door, shouting, let me oot let me oot the rabbits have got me the rabbits hiv made me bleed they've got my face they've started licking my face. They'd always come in darkness. Kill them for me, Mummy. Kill them for me. She'd plead. I cannae see the fucking things, deary, I'd say. If you can't kill them, then kill me. I wid if I could see them, deary, I'd say. Afraid of the dark she wis. Afraid of the rabbits she wis. Said they bruised her and scratched her and cut her. But I think we both ken she did it tae herself. She wis never a happy lassie. Nivver once did I see her smile.

JAMIE. I hivnae seen the rabbits.

GRANNY. And when I unlocked her door and switched the light on –

JAMIE. You locked her door.

GRANNY. And when she unlocked her door. And switched her light on. She'd be there on the flair. A big bruised forehead, where she'd been smashing it off the wall. Eventually, unfortunately, we had tae tie her tae the bed. All that wall abuse wis damaging the paintwork.

JAMIE. You tied her tae the bed.

GRANNY. So dinnae tell me you hivnae seen the rabbits, Jamie. You're jist like her. Och, you dinnae ken whit she put me through. The suffering. Starting wi the pain of her birth. My body wis nivver the same again. Your granddad nivver touched me aifter that. Could barely look at me. Nae a poke for thirty-odd year and all I hiv tae look forward tae is a prolapse. Let that be a lesson tae you.

Beat.

Come and gie your granny a hug.

JAMIE. No.

GRANNY. I put this card – whit d'you mean no?

JAMIE. No.

GRANNY. Och, awa and slit your wrists, deary.

JAMIE. Why dinnae you slit my wrists, Granny?

GRANNY. Och, go back tae your counting, Jamie.

JAMIE. She smiled.

GRANNY. Keep counting, Jamie.

JAMIE. She smiled at me.

GRANNY. Keep counting the scars on your mither's arms.

JAMIE. She must've loved me!

GRANNY. Keep counting the pills she swallowed.

JAMIE. She smiled. She splashed me. She threw her heed back and laughed.

GRANNY. Keep counting the drops of blood that spilled fae
her wrists.

JAMIE. She smiled! She splashed me! She threw her heed back
and laughed!

Beat.

Getting ready for school, I tuck my grey shirt intae my
troosers. Put my socks on. One's white. One's not white. I
can't tie my tie yet and my shoelaces hiv knots in. Granny
tied them too tight. I canter doon the hallway with my tie and
my shoes. I think Mummy's in the bathroom, I heard the
water move. She's lying in the bath, face all under. Mummy
Mummy. Can you tie my tie and unknot my knots? She lifts
her heed up. The pink water drip-dripping off her hair. She
smiles. Like a sleepy princess. No school today, silly. It's
Saturday, silly billy. She smiles. She splashes me. She throws
her heed back and laughs.

Beat.

Doorbell goes. Mummy's smile stopped. It dropped.

Door opens, it's Granny and Granddad. Granddad grips my
arm and pulls me away. Granny's got Mummy's pills in her
hand. Perhaps we're going tae the park. But I've got none
shoes on. He disnae seem tae care. I turn tae look at Mummy.
But Granny's shut the bathroom door.

Sound of bathroom door slamming.

Scene Fourteen

JAMIE *rests on his step with a blanket around him. He glances
towards the sky.*

JAMIE. Please, stars. Come oot.

*The Skinners' door quietly opens. A small blue suitcase is
placed on the step.* BUNNY *appears, searching for*

something in her handbag. She notices JAMIE. *Hoping he is asleep, she tiptoes in and closes the door.*

JAMIE. Hello, Bunny.

Pause.

Bunny? I saw you.

BUNNY (*slowly opens the door*). Shh.

She winks and tiptoes down the step, gently lifts her suitcase and begins to march off.

JAMIE (*jumping up*). Wait! Far you going?

Runs to grab her arm.

BUNNY. I'm jist popping oot.

JAMIE. Wi a suitcase?

BUNNY. Keep your voice doon. You'll wake George-Michael.

JAMIE. Far you going?!

BUNNY. I've left a wee note.

JAMIE. But… No!

He dives towards her and hugs her ankles.

Dinnae leave, Bunny!

BUNNY (*trying to kick him away*). Get off! I hiv tae go!

JAMIE. You hiv tae stay!

He bites her ankles.

This disnae happen! You're going tae stay!

BUNNY *frees herself from his grip, she has placed her suitcase centre stage.*

BUNNY. Look, Jamie. Seeing you here wi all your pooters and shite, emersed in the things you love. Well it made me think.

Beat.

So I'm off tae Japan. The hame of karaoke.

JAMIE. Whit?

BUNNY. I'm nae a whorey old moth, Jamie. I'm a beautiful butterfly.

JAMIE. But, Bunny –

BUNNY *touches his face – momentarily disabling him.*

BUNNY. She'll always be with you, Jamie. She's here right now.

Looking at me through your big blue eyes.

She exits.

JAMIE. Bunny… you forgot your…

He stares at the blue suitcase.

Scene Fifteen

Some time later. JAMIE *sits on the caravan step, startled by the noise that comes from the Skinners' caravan, a noise of things being smashed and thrown about, muffled shouting from* GEORGE-MICHAEL.

GEORGE-MICHAEL (*off*). MUM! Jesus Christ! How could you, you fuckin bitch.

Continuous crashing about.

Whit the hell am I supposed tae dae noo. Far the fuck have you gone. Jesus Christ. If I ever find you. We were a team. A fuckin good team. Who's goin tae dance wi me noo? Yiv left me. I'm all alane. Oh my God, I'm all alane. Oh my God. Oh my God. Oh my God.

More banging. JAMIE *goes to knock, but* GEORGE-MICHAEL *opens the door before his fist touches it.* GEORGE-MICHAEL *pops his head out, calmly.*

Can I help?

JAMIE. You okay?

GEORGE-MICHAEL. Fine, thanks.

JAMIE. She's gone.

GEORGE-MICHAEL. Aye.

JAMIE. Tae Japan.

GEORGE-MICHAEL. It disnae matter far a person goes,
Jamie. It's the fact that they arenae here is all we need. You
drink a lot of milk, Jamie. It's good. It maks you stronger,
doesn't it, Jamie. Maks you stronger on the inside. Maks you
closer tae your mither's breast.

*He opens the door wide to reveal him wearing a pink
cardigan and tweed skirt.*

What's the matter, Jamie? You look... different.

Moving towards JAMIE. JAMIE *is in shock.*

It's your eyes. Your eyes are different. Your eyes are... I
always thought you wis a... but you arenae. You arenae at all.

Smiles.

So, you let her go.

JAMIE. No, I... I didn't!

GEORGE-MICHAEL. You let her go.

JAMIE. No. I tried tae –

GEORGE-MICHAEL. It's how it should be, Jamie. She isnae a
whorey old moth, Jamie. She's a beautiful butterfly.

JAMIE. That's whit she said.

He hears a loud flutter of wings.

GEORGE-MICHAEL. So, I wis at the beach yesterday. Your
influence.

Smiles.

And I seen this funny looking fat dog. With no ears and flat
legs.

JAMIE. A seal.

GEORGE-MICHAEL. It looked really funny. The funniest-looking dog I've ever seen.

A loud fluttering of wings. BUNNY, dressed in a pink cardigan and tweed skirt, stands behind GEORGE-MICHAEL. She is drenched from head to toe, with seaweed caught round her shoulders.

JAMIE. Bunny.

GEORGE-MICHAEL turns around. They look at each other.

GEORGE-MICHAEL. Mum.

BUNNY. I'm sorry, baby. I couldnae dae it. I couldnae leave you.

I'm sorry for even thinking aboot it.

A loud flutter of wings as GRANNY appears.

GEORGE-MICHAEL. I'm jist glad you're back.

BUNNY. Come and gie your granny a hug.

GEORGE-MICHAEL. I put this cardigan on specially.

A loud flutter of wings.

GRANNY. That's what we grannies do. We wrap ourselves up in pink fluffy cardigans to make it a little easier for you to hug the death that is Granny.

JAMIE. Granny.

GRANNY laughs. The following three speeches overlap each other. The sound of fluttering wings continues. BUNNY and GEORGE-MICHAEL look like they are moving slowly toward JAMIE, but are actually walking towards each other, eventually open-armed.

GRANNY. Come and gie your granny a hug. I put this cardigan on specially. That's what we grannies do. We wrap ourselves up in pink fluffy cardigans to make it a little easier for you to hug the rattling death that is Granny.

BUNNY. D'you want Granny to tuck you into bed and give you a pill to make your nasty headache go away? A sugar-coated pill. Maks everything a little easier to swallow, doesn't it?

GEORGE-MICHAEL. Well, come and gie your granny a kiss then. It's a shame aboot Granny's arsehole breath, isn't it? We do try to disguise the smell with Dundee Cake. We do try.

GEORGE-MICHAEL and BUNNY have met and are smiling euphorically. GEORGE-MICHAEL holds BUNNY's hands in his and kisses them. A low buzzing noise begins and gradually gets louder. GEORGE-MICHAEL plants a line of kisses up BUNNY's arm. A louder flutter of wings. When GEORGE-MICHAEL reaches the top of BUNNY's arm, they look each other in the eyes. He nuzzles and kisses her neck. She moans. They kiss.

JAMIE. Um, guys…

The fluttering and buzzing noise is very loud.

Guys, whit are yous daein? You're family.

GEORGE-MICHAEL and BUNNY suddenly stop and stare at JAMIE.

GEORGE-MICHAEL. Family?

They both laugh.

BUNNY. We're barely the same species.

They both laugh and disappear into their caravan. The buzzing and fluttering sound becomes overwhelming. Silence.

JAMIE. Why did you take her away from me?

GRANNY. Ay?

JAMIE. You took her away. Why?

GRANNY. Well, I've nivver heard such –

The buttons fall off her cardigan.

Oh, my buttons. She asked for it. She asked me to.

JAMIE. No. You went in with her pills.

GRANNY. She asked me to.

JAMIE. No. You shut the door.

GRANNY. Did you hear her scream, Jamie? Did you hear her scream?

JAMIE. You killed her.

GRANNY. If you dinnae believe me, ask her yoursel.

JAMIE. How can I? She's gone.

GRANNY. She's closer than you think.

JAMIE. But she's dead. Just like you.

GRANNY. I may be old but I'm very much alive, you cheeky wee fuck.

Her arm falls off.

Oh shite.

JAMIE. Granny's nae here.

GRANNY *screams as she disappears into a blackout.*

JAMIE *stares at the Skinners' caravan door, his speech improvised around the following.*

George-Michael? (*Clears throat.*) George-Michael? Bunny?

Knocks lightly on door. Then harder. Pauses. He pushes the door gently. It falls to the ground. He goes in.

Far are you?

Inquisitively walks around the caravan set, through any invisible walls. There is no sign of their presence or indeed any sign of them ever being there. He goes into his caravan. It is empty. No GRANNY. *No furniture. He goes to dig up a flower box with his hands. He realises the soil and flowers are fake.*

Far are yous?

He crawls along the floor, feeling the cold and hard surface, until he finds himself face to face with the blue suitcase. He pauses. He nervously unzips the suitcase. It falls open. It is empty.

JAMIE *stands centre. His breathing is amplified, then silence.*

JAMIE. Mum?

VOICE. *Shh.*

JAMIE. I'm sorry I – I didnae go in.

VOICE. *Shh. There, there.*

JAMIE. I didnae save you. I'm sorry I –

VOICE. *Every breath was one too many*

JAMIE. He pulled me away, grip was too tight

VOICE. *Small steps felt like earthquakes*

JAMIE. She had your special pills

VOICE. *Every blink tried to keep eyes shut*

JAMIE. You wisnae supposed tae go

VOICE. *Had to leave*

JAMIE. She made you leave

VOICE. *Just gave a push*

JAMIE. But she – I thought you loved me

VOICE. *Was not well*

JAMIE. You wis happy. You smiled.

VOICE. *Had to go.*

JAMIE. But if you wis ill, how wid you ken?

Silence.

But I wis only wee

Pause.

We could've went tae the beach. We could've went tae the beach every day. You liked the beach. We went all the time. You liked it when we went in the cold mornings in our pyjamas, before it wis properly light. You said tae count the different things I could see in the rock pools. Like count to infinity. While you walked towards the sea. In your blue pyjamas. You loved the sea. You must've. You'd walk in for miles and miles and stay there for hours and hours. I'd sometimes wave at you, but I dinnae think you ever saw me. You wis too far away. And you'd nivver look back. And sometimes you'd put your heed under, then I couldnae see you at all. Like you didnae wint tae come oot. You loved the sea. Wis like you nivver winted tae come oot.

Pause.

But you always did come oot.

Pause.

And now I see. The salt water made your tears seem... smaller. Your pain seem... less. Your body seem... paler. Almost made you... disappear.

Pause.

Disappear.

Pause.

I think I'll go tae the beach. I think I'll tak a walk in the sea.

The End.

THE IMPORTANCE OF BEING ALFRED

Louise Welsh

Louise Welsh is the author of four novels: *The Cutting Room*, *Tamburlaine Must Die*, *The Bullet Trick* and *Naming the Bones* (all published by Canongate Books). Louise has written many short stories and produced features for most of the major British broadsheets. *The Importance of Being Alfred* was shortlisted for a Critics' Award for Best New Play, 2006. Her other plays include *Panic Patterns* (Citizens Theatre, 2010) and *Memory Cells* (The Arches, 2009). Louise has been the recipient of several awards and international fellowships. Her work has been translated into twenty languages. She lives in Glasgow with the author Zoë Strachan.

The Importance of Being Alfred was first performed at Òran Mór, Glasgow, as part of the A Play, a Pie and a Pint season on 17 October 2005, with the following cast:

ALFRED	Benny Young
BOSIE	James Mackenzie
PEMBERTON BILLING	Richard Conlon

Director	Liz Carruthers
Designer	Annette Gillies

242

Characters

LORD ALFRED DOUGLAS (A), *a tall, thin, raddled, but austerely elegant man of fifty*

BOSIE (B), *a handsome undergraduate of twenty-one*

PEMBERTON BILLING (PB), *a bluff, athletic man of thirty-eight*

Characters should be played as straight as possible

Author's Note

In 1918, Hugh Pemberton Billing, Independent MP for East Hertfordshire, was sued for criminal libel by the dancer Maud Allan. The trial followed accusations in Billing's proto-fascist newspaper *The Vigilante* that Allan was a lesbian German agent who was 'corrupting' prominent members of society, with a view to bribing them into undermining the war effort. One of Pemberton Billing's keenest supporters was Lord Alfred Douglas, best known as the lover of Oscar Wilde, but in later life an ardent homophobe and anti-Semite. The action of the play takes place in the run-up to the libel trial.

The year is 1918. LORD ALFRED DOUGLAS*'s sitting room.*
Afghan rugs, tasselled standard lamp, antimacassars, stuffy
Victorian atmosphere. Lights up on BOSIE, *a slender good-*
looking blond youth sitting in an armchair, reading a beautifully
bound slim volume. We get the impression that the book is not
occupying his full attention. The youth is dressed as if for
summer and has a green carnation in his buttonhole. Next to his
chair is an elegant occasional table; on it are another couple of
fine bound books and a glass containing a large measure of
malt. A second identical chair and occasional table faces his.
Behind the small seating area is a desk scattered with papers
and pens, and holding a reading lamp, a decanter of whisky and
some glasses. A combined coat and umbrella stand is stage left.
The youth sighs, leans back in the chair, stretching out his legs
and places the book on his chest. A, *a man in his fifties, enters*
stage left carrying some printed papers. He's dressed for winter
and carrying an umbrella, he has just come in from a shower of
rain. Everything about A *is ultra-conservative and yet there is a*
dapper quality to his sobriety, everything is just so. He places
his papers on the desk, shakes the umbrella, puts it in the stand,
unfastens his coat and hangs it up. A *is raising his hat from his*
head when he notices the visitor. He freezes, looking at the
youth who half rises from his chair, pleased to be interrupted
from his reading.

A. I thought I refused to see you.

B (*lowers himself back into his chair*). Perhaps if you closed
your eyes…?

A goes to the desk and gets himself a drink, the mirror of his
companion's.

A. Perhaps if I promise you a beating?

B. I'd consider that a poor incentive.

A. I'm not trying to reward you.

B. Don't you think that laying your hands on me, getting yourself all... worked up would make me even more present? That's supposing you can lay your hands on me.

A *lifts a walking stick from the coat stand.*

(*Coolly.*) Feel free to try.

A *looks between the walking stick and* B *as if considering attack, then throws it back into the stand.*

A. Why are you here?

B. I've got to be somewhere, why not here?

A. Because you're not wanted.

B. I wouldn't be here if that were true.

A (*with emphasis*). You are not welcome.

B. You can't take your eyes off me.

A. I want you to leave.

B. If you meant that I'd go. (*Relaxed.*) Sit down, drink your drink, it's excellent whisky.

A. What do you want?

B *ignores him, goes to the desk and lifts one of the papers* A *was carrying when he entered. Reads out its title.*

B. *The Vigilante.*

A. The newspaper of patriots.

B. The last refuge of scoundrels?

A. The organ of choice for right-thinking men.

B. Really? (*Begins to read.*) 'There exists in the *cabinet noir* of a certain German Prince a book compiled by the Secret Service from reports of German agents who have infested this country for the past twenty years, agents so vile and spreading such debauchery and such lasciviousness as only German minds can conceive and only German bodies execute.' Do you believe that?

A. Every word. Except for the part about debauchery only being executed by German bodies. Sadly that is mistaken.

B (*raises his eyebrows. Continues reading*). 'In the beginning of the book is a précis of general instructions regarding the propagation of evils which all decent men thought had perished in Sodom and Lesbia. There are the names of forty-seven thousand men and women, Privy Councillors, wives of Cabinet Ministers, even Cabinet Ministers themselves, diplomats, poets, bankers, editors, newspaper proprietors and members of His Majesty's Household prevented from putting their full strength into the war by corruption, blackmail and fear of exposure.' (*Looks sceptical.*)

A. It's a fact.

B. You believe that there are forty-seven thousand amongst our great and good who have been corrupted by German agents and are being blackmailed into undermining the war effort? (*Laughs.*) I didn't realise we had forty-seven thousand great and good available to be perverted.

A. Then you are naive.

B. No, I thought that all the great and good had submitted to corruption long before the war ever started.

A. You think you're amusing.

B *shrugs.*

This is no laughing matter.

Becomes schoolteacherish. This is something that has been explained to him and he's taking pleasure at explaining it in turn.

Britain is the most upstanding nation in the world. And yet after three years of war our troops are still languishing in the trenches. Why?

B. You tell me.

A *takes a seat and leans forward earnestly.*

A. Have you ever walked round Marble Arch or Hyde Park Corner at twilight?

B (*rests himself on the arm of the chair opposite*). Once or twice, when I've been in the mood.

A. Then you'll have seen agents of the Kaiser loitering in the shadows. (*Mimics camp voice.*) ''Scuse me, sir, 'ave you got a light?' And should you offer them a light, what next?

B. They smoke their cigarette?

A. They engage you in conversation. They propose a drink, then once they've built fellow feeling with talk and alcohol, they suggest retirement to a quiet room where you can converse in peace. Or perhaps, if they judge you to be of a garrulous temperament, they'll know of a party where a man at a loose end might find convivial company. These are highly trained operatives willing to stoop to anything. I've explored the shadows of London and seen them, primping, pouting, flaunting themselves shamelessly. I know of parties where thirty or forty men have danced together – (*Whispers.*) some of them dressed as women.

B (*drops down into the chair*). You get about. Walk around after dark a lot, do you?

A. It sickens me.

B. The way too much candy sickens.

A (*gets to his feet*). The way the stench of shit forces you to gag. Why are there still Germans who are allowed to walk free in England while over in France their countrymen are fighting our troops?

B (*relaxed*). Why not? They prefer our way of life, why should they want to destroy it?

A. Pssssssh. The enemy wants to worm its way through what is brightest and best in our country. They hide among us, pretending to have taken on our ways while all the time they are a cancer eating away at all that is good. Why are German banks still allowed to operate on our soil? Why does so much of the nation's wealth lie in Jewish hands? Why are we losing the war?

B *shrugs, goes to the drinks cabinet and tops up his whisky.*

Because those who could make a difference are being black-mailed by the German Secret Service. We're failing on the western front because of the pernicious influence of the enemy within.

B. Within what?

A. Within the very upper echelons of society.

B. Personally, I've always found the upper echelons rather ugly.

A. These are the cream of our fighting forces. Men who have been bred to lead us to victory. They've had their strengths honed on the playing fields of England and their minds sharpened at Oxford and Cambridge. The Kaiser doesn't find them ugly.

B. Each to his own.

A *grabs a scrap of paper from the desk and reads the final six lines of the poem* All's Well With England, *then triumphantly flings the paper back on the desk as if he has proved a point.*

Your own composition?

A. The climax of my epic poem *All's Well With England.* The title is ironic.

B. Pure doggerel.

A. People who know poetry admire my verse. (*Pulls himself together as if realising what he's doing.*) Why am I talking to you?

B. You find me charming. It's not uncommon.

A. I find you disgusting. Get out.

B *ignores him.*

In the name of Christ and all that is holy, I demand that you go.

B (*looks skywards as if listening*). I don't think he heard you.

A (*slight desperation*). Please leave, I'm expecting a visitor.

B. A fallen serviceman in need of succour?

A. A man of honour and brilliance.

B. I'd like to meet him.

A. Impossible.

B. If it's possible for you, then I imagine it will be possible for me.

A. You are fucking presumptuous.

B. And you are fashioning a hell for yourself.

A. What would you know of hell?

B. Less than you.

A. If I know hell it's because I have suffered for my sins and if I know about virtue it's because I am trying to redeem myself.

B. What you call sin is nothing and what you consider virtues are nothing too.

A. Get thee behind me, Satan.

B (*puts himself lewdly behind* A). Is that what you say to these secret agents lurking around Hyde Park Corner?

   A *tries to catch* B *and is nimbly outmanoeuvred.*

A. What are you?

   During the next few lines, A *and* B*'s movements are mirrors of each other.*

B. You know me.

A. No I don't.

B. You deny me?

A. I don't know you.

B. That's twice. Will there be a third time?

A. And a fourth and a fifth and as many times as I have to before you accept that I do not know you nor do I wish to.

B. Oh, you liar, Alfred. Come on, say my name.

A. I will not recognise you. Go. You have no business here.

Mirroring stops, B *sinks back into his chair and takes a drink.*

B (*disappointed*). Everything is business with you now. Do you remember when you would go out on a spree and find yourself amongst the poorest people in the city, in a music hall somewhere, soaking up drink and simple pleasures, like Shakespeare and all the great poets did in their day? You were a poet then. Do you remember?

A (*sulkily defensive*). I am still a poet.

B. You're a versifier, nothing more. But in those days... (*Sighs as he looks into the golden past.*) Do you remember? You'd walk through the meanest parts of town, poverty and depravity winking at you from every alley, every doorway. Some of your companions were too frightened to accompany you, but you were as much in love with the risk as you were with the performance. Do you recall the night that big fellow attacked you?

A. No.

B. He was skulking in a doorway, a big brute of a man with his cap pulled low over his eyes. You hardly had any warning, just a ghost of something moving in the corner of your eye, then he was upon you. (*Softly entreating.*) Remember.

A (*slowly, as if just remembering*). He thought he could best me because I was alone and dressed like a gentleman. (*Enthusiastically.*) I caught him a right hook to the head then, when he was down, lay into him with my stick and my boots. (*Demonstrates.*) Ha! He was a big brute, taller than me, that's certain, but once he was in the dirt there was no recovery for him. My shoes may have been handmade, but they were steel-capped. His ribs snapped like dry kindling.

B. He curled himself into a knot, pleading for a mercy he would never have shown you. You raised your foot and aimed at his head. (*Acts the preparation to a kick.*) In that moment you held the power of death in you.

A. A crowd had gathered. They seemed awed, but I knew their admiration might turn ugly, the poor can become wicked when the rich win. I pulled back my kick, tipped my hat to the women and walked swiftly to the theatre.

B. Why let that cur spoil your plans?

A. Why indeed?

B. The hall was pressed full of people. There was a smell of smoke and sweat, cheap lavender water and excitement. A woman whispered something to you and ran a finger down the line of your spine. You shoved her away, grabbed a drink, went up to the balcony and met up with some other young blades.

A. They asked about the mud on my cape and I made some jest.

B. They should have seen the other chap!

A. Then the footlights flared and suddenly everything was drowned in a turmoil of applause.

B. The master of ceremonies stepped forth in his shabby evening suit and the crowd cheered.

A. You could lose yourself in the crush and the cheering.

B. Then the show began. Do you remember? (*Sings*.)
    'The boy I love is up in the gallery,
    The boy I love is looking down at me,
    There he is, can't you see, waving with his handkerchief.'

BOTH. 'As merry as a robin that sings in a tree.'

Sound of footsteps, someone being admitted to the house from offstage.

PB (*shouting from offstage*). Lord Alfred? (*Enters and looks about him.*) Do you have company?

A. Mr Pemberton Billing. No. I'm alone. I was just clearing my throat.

B *tops up his drink, then leans against the desk, sipping it and watching the others.*

PB. Getting in good voice for the fight ahead, eh?

A *is slightly blustering, he makes a good recovery, but is aware of* B*'s presence.*

A. I'm ready for whatever the enemy cares to throw at us. Can I offer you a drink?

PB. A whisky would be most welcome, thank you. (*Settles himself in* A'*s chair.*) But the question might more rightly be – what are we going to throw at them?

A *shoves* B, *who merely looks amused. None of this is observed by* PB *who is making himself comfortable.*

A. The black book, the forty-seven thousand.

PB. More perhaps.

A *hands* PB *his drink, but is reluctant to take his own seat and have his back to* B, *so hovers with his arms on the back of the second chair.*

A. I don't doubt it. I wouldn't be surprised to find out there were one hundred thousand who were being blackmailed by the enemy.

PB. Indeed – (*Drinks with obvious enjoyment.*) but that wasn't quite my point. There was a reason that I asked to see you tonight.

A. Yes?

PB. We have to rethink our strategy. The black book alone isn't going to be enough.

A (*incredulous*). But it's a scandal of the highest proportions.

PB. We must face facts. Our campaign is failing to take hold. Even as men at the front sacrifice themselves for the Empire, there are those who laugh at the notion of forty-seven thousand homosexuals undermining our war effort.

B (*sarcastic*). Surely not.

PB (*looks at* A). Did you say something?

A. No, I mean I said '*surely not*'.

PB. Hard for an upstanding man to believe, I know, but yes, the British public laughs, while meanwhile the most sordid depravities are played out in the trenches between men who should be ripping the guts out of the Hun with their bayonets.

B (*makes an enthusiastic bayoneting movement*). Sticking them right through.

PB. Are you unwell, Lord Alfred?

A. No, perfectly well. Just a little disturbed by this shocking development.

PB. Don't worry, we're not beaten yet. This is just a small battle, a mere skirmish, in a long war. Have a seat.

A *reluctantly takes a seat,* B *rests his arms on the back of it, eagerly observing the conversation,* PB *leans forward intensely.*

The public don't credit the truth of the forty-seven thousand precisely because it *is* so big. The man in the street is too simple to envisage that so many of his betters can have fallen so utterly and so disgracefully. We need to show them the levels of depravity that exist by making an example of an individual.

A. You have at least forty-seven thousand to choose from.

PB. Exactly, and there is one that fits our purposes perfectly. A person who has been corrupted in the salons of Berlin. A person fêted by society, a person who has even visited the home of the ex-Prime Minister.

A (*with vitriol*). The Prime Bugger.

PB. We will take this person and crucify them on the altar of their perversion.

A. Who is he?

PB. She. Maud Allan is to give a private performance of Oscar Wilde's *Salome*.

B (*sombre*). A tragedy in one act.

A (*with passion, he has forgotten* B*'s presence*). The lord of abominations. Wilde was the greatest force of evil to appear in Europe during the last three-hundred-and-fifty years. Prosecution, exile, death even don't stop him assaulting the nation's morality.

B (*sadly*). You have turned into that well-known ass, your father.

PB. Wilde's influence has met its match. I've had an article prepared that will bring Maud Allan to her knees.

B (*sings with increasing lewdness*).
'Come into the garden, Maud,
For the black bat, night, has flown –'

A. A position in which she's no doubt spent much of her time.

PB. No doubt.

B. 'Come into the garden, Maud,
I am here at the gate alone.'

Throughout the scene, A desperately tries to ignore B. PB cannot see him, but is increasingly aware of A's agitation.

PB. We will bring news of her outrages before the public. Let them judge her. It has been done before.

A. I remember.

PB. How could you forget?

B. Do you remember the letter he sent you from prison? 'De Profundis' – from the depths.

A. It was in a different life. But I don't suppose I'll ever forget.

B stands to the right of the others with his back straight.

B. 'Everything about my tragedy has been hideous, mean, repellent, lacking in style; our very dress makes us grotesque. We are the zanies of sorrow. We are clowns whose hearts are broken.'

PB. The headline will read: 'The Cult of the Clitoris'.

A. Clitoris? A Greek term?

B. 'On November 13th, 1895, I was brought down here from London. From two o'clock till half-past two on that day I had to stand on the centre platform of Clapham Junction in convict dress, and handcuffed, for the world to look at.'

PB. Yes, Greek – the root of all these outrages seems to lie in that country.

A. Classics is a dangerous subject for any young man to study. I'm unfamiliar with the word 'clitoris'. What does it refer to?

PB. It is an anatomical term – I got it from a doctor of my acquaintance. The cult of the clitoris is the female equivalent of sodomy. It takes medical training or an exceptionally depraved mind to work out the mechanics.

B. 'Of all possible objects I was the most grotesque. When people saw me they laughed. Nothing could exceed their amusement. That was, of course, before they knew who I was.'

PB. I've had an announcement prepared for *The Vigilante*.

Takes a piece of paper out of his pocket and begins to read.

'To be a member of Maud Allan's private performance in Oscar Wilde's *Salome* one has to apply to Miss Valetta of 9 Duke Street, Adelphi, WC. If Scotland Yard were to seize the list of these members, I have no doubt they would secure the names of several of the first forty-seven thousand.'

A. The authorities should take the audience to court and prosecute them as the sods they are. Jail is too good for them.

B. 'As soon as they discovered my identity they laughed still more. For half an hour I stood there in the grey November rain surrounded by a jeering mob.'

A *gets to his feet and speaks with quiet but intense anger.*

A. Let crowds jeer. Let every form of humiliation fall on the queers and inverts. Let them be ridiculed, pilloried. Put them in the stocks, birch them, hang them in the marketplace. Put them up against the wall and shoot them as traitors to the war, to their country and to God.

B. 'For a year after that was done to me I wept every day at the same hour and for the same space of time.'

A (*sadly, sinking back into his chair*). I have wept too.

PB. What?

A (*remembers himself*). It makes me weep.

PB. England weeps. The best of her youth sacrifice themselves in the mud of France while the other half drift into decadence. But not for long. I promise you, Lord Alfred, we will win this battle and those embroiled in decadence will be marched off to fight an honest fight. War will cleanse England of Jews, Germans, homosexuals and depravity. All those enemies currently skulking within our borders will be rooted out and England will return to the greatness that is her right.

Knocks back the last of his drink as if drinking a toast, and slams the empty glass on the table.

A (*gets up and refills his and* PB*'s glass*). I tried to join up when war was declared. They said I was too old.

B (*looks with dismay at his empty glass*). Too earnest.

PB. Your talents are being put to better use than they ever could be in France.

A. Perhaps – (*Hands* PB *his glass and takes a sip from his own.*) but I would have liked the chance to do my bit.

B (*grabs umbrella from the stand and mimics a soldier*). Striding at the head of the parade, your uniform cut at one of London's better tailors, your chin thrust upwards, bayonet flashing against the sun. And behind you a shining column of gilded manhood, each one bolder than the last, resting their rifles on their broad shoulders, their muscular chests pumped full of pride.

B *sings the first four lines of 'Wish Me Luck as You Wave Me Goodbye' by Harry Parr-Davies.*

A *stands with the erect bearing of a soldier. Gazes into his imagination.*

A. I would have steered the youths in my command in the path of righteousness. They would have no wish to stray from the guidance of my firm hand.

B (*flings the umbrella back into the stand*). You would return purged if not purified.

PB. You may get your chance yet. I hear the War Office is thinking of raising the age of conscription. Perhaps they could give you a post in their offices.

A. I have no desire to push a pen.

B. No, you want to fire your big gun.

A. I want to face the enemy.

B. Cheek to cheek.

PB. An admirable ambition, but the security of the homeland must not be neglected. Bloody stupid to send a man of your abilities to France to be gallantly dispatched on his first day.

A. What could be better than dying for your country beside men that you love?

B. Living with the man that you love.

PB. My advisors say that if I publish an article about her role as high priestess in the cult of the clitoris, Maud Allan will be forced to sue me for libel.

A (*looking at* B). A fucking outrage!

PB. Yes, but it's precisely the step that we want her to take. Remember, once she is in court we can force the public to listen to the perversion in her private life and not-so-private performances. Once they hear the details, the press will have a field day, there won't be a man or woman in England left in ignorance about the goings-on in the salons of the elite. Let them deny the existence of the Kaiser's agents then. Let them ignore the truth of the forty-seven thousand at their peril.

B. How ugly you've grown. 'People talk of secret vices. There are no such things.

He leans forward and touches A*'s face, tracing the lines he sees there, finally holding* A*'s hands gently in his while* A *stares at him with half-hypnotised horror.*

If a wretched man has a vice it shows itself in the lines of his mouth, the droop of his eyelids, the moulding of his hands even.'

A (*shakes himself free of* B*'s grip*). Horrible fiend, phantasm.

PB (*looking at* A). Are you sure that you are quite well, Lord Alfred? You seem a little out of sorts.

A *hesitates, looking at* B.

B. Answer him, are you feeling a trifle queer?

A. I'm appalled that a woman could be so debauched.

PB. Oh, she's a habitual debaucher with an unnatural fascination for all that is dark. May I?

He takes out his cigarette packet. A *nods,* PB *offers him one and they both light up.* PB*'s fascination with Maud's exotic performance should be reminiscent of* A*'s homoerotic attraction towards the soldiers.*

She dances near naked, her uncovered breasts strung with pearls, her hair wild and untamed. Gold and silver bracelets rattle on her wrists and ankles. She looks like a wanton savage. In her hands she carries a tray on which rests the severed head of John the Baptist. It is a wax copy, but finely done, I'm told. She whirls faster and faster, dropping one flimsy veil after another, staring with open lust into the grotesque thing's eyes. Then, as if all the rest were not outrage enough, at the end of the dance she raises its mouth to her lips. She kisses it. His severed head! When she danced at Covent Garden they decided it was too obscene and substituted a dish of gravy.

B. He fancies himself as John the Baptist, but looks more like the dish of gravy.

A. It is beyond belief.

PB. She comes from bad blood. Her brother was a rival to Jack the Ripper. He killed two young girls, then left their naked, abused bodies in a church.

PB *is visibly titillated, caught between horror and delight.*

A. Horrible.

PB. His first victim they found in a cupboard. Police had searched the entire building but they overlooked this particular cubbyhole because it seemed too small to hold a body. It was only when they saw the blood dripping through the door that they opened it and made their gruesome discovery. Maud's brother Theo had solved the problem of space. He had hacked the poor girl to pieces with an axe.

A (*fascinated*). And the second victim?

PB. He laid her out naked on a table in the basement, as if preparing for a medical examination. She had wounds on her body too terrible to contemplate. And what do you suppose Miss Allan's reaction was to her brother's crime?

A. Any normal woman would be filled with horror.

PB. She wrote to the court from Berlin, Berlin mark you, begging that he be spared the rope.

B. So she is bad because her brother was bad. Your mother divorced your father because of his insanity, your poor brother killed himself and your son is heading towards the asylum. If she is stained by her family, then so are you.

A (*looking at* B). Unnatural creature.

PB. Unnatural indeed. She has held women-only performances of Salome's Dance of the Seven Veils, where the audience are invited to come dressed as she does, like the Whore of Babylon. Can you see them? Gathered round dressed in wisps of oriental fabric, while in their centre Miss Maud gyrates, slowly peeling back each veil, one by one, until she is writhing on the floor – (*Does an unconscious move of the hips.*) naked. I have tried to persuade the porter at the club to conceal me in a cupboard so I can document the orgiastic climax to this coven, but he refused my bribe. Now that I think on it, there was a dark cast to his eye, he was very possibly Jewish, a Jewish invert.

A. The scene defies my powers of imagination.

B. There's a surprise.

PB. Oh, I can see it clearly in my mind's eye. It makes my blood run cold.

A. She's attempting to pervert British womanhood in the service of the Kaiser.

PB. There's no doubt about it. By turning women towards the cult of the clitoris, she is as responsible for the emasculation of the British serviceman as Oscar Wilde himself. We'll deal her a dose of the same medicine that fixed him.

A. You're certain she'll sue you for libel?

PB. I guarantee it.

A. And you're sure of success?

PB. The truth is no slander.

B (*sadly resigned*). History will repeat itself. Art and love will be on trial.

PB. I'll conduct my own defence. It will be magnificent. I'll thrust Maud Allan before the entire country. She will be forced to face me and listen to a catalogue of her perversions. I will stop those naked feet from dancing and teach her that there is a hard price to pay for defying decency.

B. It can be as low as five shillings.

A. This price will be high.

PB (*self-consciously casual*). Do you think she'll attend court in costume?

A. Who knows what she is capable of.

PB. Who indeed? (*Rubs his hands.*) So you are with me, Alfred? You'll support me when Maud Allan sues?

A. With everything that I have.

PB. Good man. I want you to be there when I show the Germans that, no matter what their secret ploys, we are still a nation of men. I'm going to nail Maud Allan in full view of the British public and show her for the conniving whore that she is. After that it's only a small step to rooting every filthy German, Jew, inverted female and sodomite out of this country. (*Looks at his watch.*) Ah well, time and tide, eh, Lord Alfred?

A (*relieved*). You have to go?

PB. I have a paper to prepare for the House, a proposition that any German nationals in this country should be denied access to air-raid shelters until British women and children are safely inside, and a demand for a special tax on all immigrants living within England.

A. Why not? There are enough of them.

PB. Exactly.

They shake hands, PB *slaps* A *exuberantly on the back.*

See you in court!

A. I pray it's so.

PB *exits stage left.*

B (*with feeling*). Odious man.

A. He's a fine patriot.

B. He's a fool. You're going to be part of this persecution, after all you've experienced?

A. It's for the good of the nation. The Government has had plenty of time to act against the threat within, and what have they come up with? The Defence of the Realm Act. (*Looks disgusted.*) This editorial will start a scandal that will force their hand.

B. This is how it all started before, with a written insult. 'To Oscar Wilde posing as a sodomite.'

A. It was the act of a concerned father desperate to save his son from corruption.

B (*scornful*). Since when was your father concerned? Since when were either of us *led* into corruption? You ran towards it at full tilt. (*Sober.*) After months of persecution, the final outrage, scrawled on a card and handed to the porter at his club. No envelope, that made it public, so Oscar was forced to sue to protect his good name.

A. The trial revealed it was no pose, no slander.

B. They humiliated him.

A. They upheld the law and prosecuted him.

B. He was sentenced to two years hard labour. But the real sentence was death.

A. It was justice.

B. To kill a man because of the object of his love?

A. You paint love in colours of silver and gold, but the trial revealed it in all its putridness. The stained sheets, the money changing hands...

B. It was the secrecy that made it sordid, not the act itself.

A. If secrecy and lies are sordid then Wilde was base a million times over. When everything was lost he declared himself for what he was. I remember his twisted letter as well as you. (*A sarcastic tone*.) 'A great friend of mine – a friend of ten years' standing – came to see me some time ago, and told me that he did not believe a single word of what was said against me, and wished me to know that he considered me quite innocent, and the victim of a hideous plot. I burst into tears at what he said, and told him that while there was much amongst the definite charges that was quite untrue and transferred to me by revolting malice, still that my life had been full of perverse pleasures, and that unless he accepted that as a fact about me and realised it to the full I could not possibly be friends with him any more, or ever be in his company. It was a terrible shock to him, but we are friends, and I have not got his friendship on false pretences.' Oh yes, once he was in exile he acknowledged his nature, but while he still had the vestiges of a reputation, he lied. He lied to his lawyers, the judge and jury, he lied to his mother, his children, his wife. It wasn't secrecy that sent Wilde to jail, it was his guilt.

B (*sadly*). We were born out of time. If we'd lived in ancient Greece our love would have been celebrated. And I know that were we to be reborn one hundred years from now we'd face none of the misery that destroyed Oscar.

A. His acts invoked a natural revulsion, it will always be so.

B. No, it's a sign of the savagery of our age. A new word has been coined for your form of hatred – homophobia. In the future it will fall out of use. It'll become an obscure term found only in antiquated dictionaries, a curiosity, a testament to our lack of civilisation. It was an injustice that Oscar had to lie. The law that forced him to deny himself is the same source that destroyed him.

A (*cruelly*). You destroyed him. You urged him to stand and fight when all his other friends, his true friends, were insistent he flee to France.

B. He wanted to go ahead as much as I did, even though he knew the risks. He was ready to accept disaster. Each man kills the thing he loves, and who did Oscar love more than himself?

A. When he could have pulled out with honour, citing lack of funds, you borrowed money and lent it to him – lent it though you'd spent half his fortune. You sentenced him as sure as any magistrate.

B. I wanted him to prove that what we felt was not diabolical.

A. When Oscar should have been forming his defence, you dragged him to Monte Carlo. He sat alone while you threw yourself into the gaming tables. You lost on every card, every spin of the roulette wheel, you should have taken it as a sign.

B. We refused to let anyone ruin our gaiety.

A. You called him a coward then, when he took the stand, turned your back on him.

B (*defensive*). I wanted to testify, but everyone was against it. I stayed in London until the night before the trial. I suffered, probably more than he did during those two long years. He was safe in jail while I had to face the world.

A. You faced them from France.

B (*more defensive*). It was as near to England as I dare. My father offered me money to go to the South Seas. He insisted I'd find women so beautiful they'd turn me from my vices.

A. Your mother summed your habits up. (*Puts on a Lady Bracknell-type voice*.) 'Brandy, betting and boys.'

B (*sadly*). Mother's vocabulary always was limited. I told my father to take his allowance to hell and took myself to France. But each time I settled I was subject to scorn. In Le Havre…

A (*wistful*). I remember…

B (*wistful*). It was a beautiful summer. It would have been an insult to nature to have sat indoors thinking of prison cells. I hired a yacht…

A. And engaged a boatman…

B. Who introduced me to some fishermen…

A. Who brought along some sailor friends…

B. We swam and sailed and fished…

A. Until the *Journal de Havre* printed an article about the young Lord of Sodom cavorting naked with local youth.

BOTH. Cunts.

B. I was true to Oscar. I wrote to him the whole time he was in jail.

A. Complaints and demands.

B. Assurances of love. I told him to be strong, that it is what we fear that happens to us.

A. And when he was released? Did he fear that you might leave him then? If he did, it was another fear realised.

B. I begged to be allowed to join him. Oscar refused to see me. He began negotiations with his wife. (*Pleased with himself*.) But she was cautious where I was reckless. She made conditions while I offered love without limits. (*Triumphant*.) In the end, he couldn't resist. I settled with him in Naples.

A. And left within the year.

B. There were problems, difficulties.

A. He had run through his money and so you went.

B. No, it was you who left, not me.

A. You decided. Your mother wrote and said she would give you an allowance if you were to return home, two hundred pounds a year was too good to resist. So you made your excuses, packed your bags and went.

B. It wasn't like that...

A. You deny the money? The allowance?

B. No, but...

A. Prison had turned him into an old man. He ended up near destitute, and even once you inherited your father's fortune you settled nothing on him. He was left to beg on the streets of Paris. (*With disgust.*) The love that dare not speak its name? The love that waits for the rustle of banknotes before it whispers its fine words.

B (*shouts*). It was you who left.

A (*quiet*). I was never there.

B. You were always there, always lurking, always whispering, putting thoughts into my head. You conspired with the world to infect me with hate. Then little by little you started to take over. The goodness in me shrank and what was left wrinkled and twisted like an unholy portrait, then one day – there you were, an old man.

A (*looks down at himself*). And here I stand. A long time ago I was you, Bosie, but then slowly I started to change, until one day I realised that I was Alfred and I wanted to smash everything I'd once worshipped. Everything you'd worshipped.

B. And with it yourself.

A (*with the even reasonableness of a madman*). Not me, you and all that are like you. Every effeminate nancy boy and muscled boatman, every unnatural woman and simpering renter. I'm glad that there are perverts in the Army. I hope every one of them gets a bullet through the heart. I hate all remembrance of you. I will cut you out of my soul.

B. You'll never destroy me. I'm there in every act of hatred, every moment of persecution, every petty act of self-delusion. You can hate and plot and demolish all that you want, but you can't quite kill me. I am the truest part of you. If I die then you die too.

A. You are nothing to me.

B. Kill me and you kill yourself.

A *lifts a knife from the drinks cabinet and lurches towards* B. B *opens up his arms and exposes his chest as a target.* A *grabs him and hesitates.*

(*Unsure.*) See, it's impossible, you can't do it.

A *and* B *hesitate,* A*'s hand still pointing the knife towards* B*'s chest, caught in mid-air. Their eyes lock and they kiss.* A *shoves* B *and the boy lands on the ground, looking up at* A *triumphant.* A *still stands over him, holding the knife, he may yet pounce.*

Lights out.

The End.